# MICHAEL J. KRUGER
# HEBREWS
# FOR YOU

**Hebrews For You**

© Michael J. Kruger, 2021

Published by:
The Good Book Company

thegoodbook.com | thegoodbook.co.uk
thegoodbook.com.au | thegoodbook.co.nz | thegoodbook.co.in

ISBN: 9781784986056

Cover design by Ben Woodcraft | Printed in India

# CONTENTS

# SERIES PREFACE

Each volume of the *God's Word For You* series takes you to the heart of a book of the Bible, and applies its truths to your heart.

The central aim of each title is to be:

- Bible centered
- Christ glorifying
- Relevantly applied
- Easily readable

You can use *Hebrews For You:*

**To read.** You can simply read from cover to cover, as a book that explains and explores the themes, encouragements and challenges of this part of Scripture.

**To feed.** You can work through this book as part of your own personal regular devotions, or use it alongside a sermon or Bible-study series at your church. Each chapter is divided into two (or occasionally three) shorter sections, with questions for reflection at the end of each.

**To lead.** You can use this as a resource to help you teach God's word to others, both in small-group and whole-church settings. You'll find tricky verses or concepts explained using ordinary language, and helpful themes and illustrations along with suggested applications.

These books are not commentaries. They assume no understanding of the original Bible languages, nor a high level of biblical knowledge. Verse references are marked in **bold** so that you can refer to them easily. Any words that are used rarely or differently in everyday language outside the church are marked in **gray** when they first appear, and are explained in a glossary toward the back. There, you'll also find details of resources you can use alongside this one, in both personal and church life.

Our prayer is that as you read, you'll be struck not by the contents of this book, but by the book it's helping you open up; and that you'll praise not the author of this book, but the One he is pointing you to.

*Carl Laferton, Series Editor*

**Bible translation used:**

ESV: English Standard Version (This is the version being quoted unless otherwise stated.)

# INTRODUCTION TO HEBREWS

The book of Hebrews gives us an extraordinary sense of clarity and wonder about Jesus. As you read, you will very quickly become aware that this author just loves Jesus Christ. He thinks he is amazing, magnificent, extraordinary. He is wonderful. He is all in all.

You might respond by saying, "I felt like that once!" It may feel like a while since you have really been gripped by the magnificence of Christ. We all experience times when we just have our nose to the grindstone, following Jesus out of duty and obligation instead of delight in how wonderful he is. At those times it is easy to look over at something else—some other person or situation or community or way of living—and think, "That looks better."

If that feeling is familiar, then the book of Hebrews is for you. It will remind you of Jesus' superiority over all things, and it will do so right from the very first verses.

As we will see, the book can be summed up in one simple phrase: Jesus is better.

Curiously, we don't know who wrote the book of Hebrews. It was likely written in the middle of the first century, probably in the early 60s AD, but no specific author is named. This uncertainty does not affect our confidence in the authority of the book. The author tells us that his message "was declared first by the Lord, and ... attested to us by those who heard" (2:3). Thus, while the author does not appear to have been an **apostle**,* the information he has given us in this book comes from the apostles themselves.

But it is the audience that really helps us to understand the book. "Hebrews" is just another name for the Jewish people. The audience appears to be primarily Jewish Christians who grew up in Judaism but have believed in Jesus. They have embraced him as the Messiah. Yet they have hit a snag. For whatever reason—perhaps the pressure of persecution and opposition—they are thinking about going

---

* Words in **gray** are defined in the Glossary (page 232).

back to Judaism. They are considering leaving this new-found faith and going back to the old ways: animal sacrifices, worship at the temple—the old paths, if you will, that Jews had trusted in for generations. In other words, these people are starting to doubt whether this Jesus thing is all it first promised to be.

**This is the major theme of the book: Jesus is better.**

Our author responds to this by showing, all through the book, how Jesus is superior to every possible thing that you could put in his place. He's superior to the angels. He's superior to the prophets. He's superior to Moses, Aaron, and Joshua. His **covenant** is superior to the old covenant. This is the major theme of the book: Jesus is better. There is nothing grander, greater, more beautiful, more wonderful, more satisfying, or more extraordinary than him.

Of course, there are probably not many readers of this expository guide who are thinking about giving up on Jesus and going back to animal sacrifices. But we are all tempted to look to other things which we suspect may be better than Jesus—whether those be work, relationships, money, or anything else. That is why the message of the book of Hebrews applies to all of us. What God gives us in the book of Hebrews is a **doctrinal** anchor: a clear and detailed understanding of exactly how and why Jesus is better than anything else. This will prevent us from drifting away from our faith.

Before embarking on this journey, you should know that the book of Hebrews is not a light appetizer. It is more like a porterhouse steak. The author talks a lot about how Jesus' sacrifice is superior to the sacrifices made in the Old Testament—requiring us to think hard about the structure and complexity of the old-covenant system. It is heavy, meaty stuff. But it's wonderful stuff.

Many of us struggle to understand the relationship between the Old Testament and the New Testament. What is the relevance of the

Old Testament? What still applies and what doesn't? How do the two Testaments link together? Did people know Jesus was coming? These are monumental questions. And the book of Hebrews answers many of those questions. It helps us to understand the overall story of the whole Bible: the entire scope of **redemptive history**. It ranges across the Old Testament and shows us how Christ fulfilled it all. He is the crescendo of God's work on earth.

In the outline of the book below, you will immediately be able to see that Christ's superiority is the key point. You can also see that, punctuating the main flow of the author's argument, there are six warnings. All of these follow the same simple theme: don't turn away from Jesus. These warnings are there to keep us walking with him on the right path—the path to life.

I.    Christ Superior to the Prophets (1:1-3)

II.   Christ Superior to the Angels (1:4 – 2:18)

      First Warning: Pay Attention (2:1-4)

III.  Christ Superior to Moses and Joshua (3:1 – 4:13)

      Second Warning: Don't be Like the Israelites in the Wilderness (3:7-19)

IV.   Christ Superior to Aaron (4:14 – 7:28)

      Third Warning: Don't Fall Away (5:11 – 6:12)

V.    Christ Superior to the Old Covenant (8:1 – 10:18)

VI.   Faith as the Superior Way of the New Covenant (10:19 – 13:19)

      Fourth Warning: Don't Keep on Sinning (10:19-39)

      Fifth Warning: Don't Miss the Grace of God (12:14-24)

      Sixth Warning: Don't Refuse to Listen to God (12:25-29)

VII.  Concluding Exhortations and Greetings (13:1-25)

The word of God is a powerful thing. The book of Hebrews tells us it is "living and active, sharper than any two-edged sword" (4:12). It can penetrate your heart and your life in ways that you never knew or thought of. It can change you, encourage you, convict you, mold you, and empower you to share the gospel with those around you.

The book of Hebrews is one we don't tend to study often in our churches. But it is in our Bible for a reason. What would we do without a book that so clearly, grandly, and magnificently proclaims the wonders of Jesus? My prayer for you as you read the book of Hebrews is that the Lord will help you to see those wonders, and most importantly, to be changed by them. I hope that, in a fresh and new way, you will fall in love with Christ all over again.

# 1. THE SON IN ALL HIS GLORY

## A Speaking God

One of the most common objections to Christianity is that God is silent. Skeptics say that, if God exists at all, he isn't really a speaking God. He is out there in the distance, disengaged from the world, and no one can be sure what he's like.

On the flip side, there are others in our world who think God speaks through anything and everything: every religion, every spiritualist, every crystal ball. There is no one channel that God speaks through primarily. It is open-ended.

The opening of the book of Hebrews refutes *both* of these views when it tells us that God "has spoken to us by his Son" (**1:2***). Contrary to the skeptic, we see that indeed God has spoken! We can know things about him. At the same time, he has not spoken in any old way. He has spoken fundamentally, fully, and finally through Jesus.

Thus, our author opens his letter with a focus on the overriding theme of the book of Hebrews: the supremacy of Christ over all things. In later chapters, our author will show that Christ is superior to angels, to **Moses**, to **Joshua**, to **Aaron**, and beyond.

But he begins by showing that Christ is the *superior revelation of God*. In the first three verses we see that Jesus is the best word from God we can get. He is the fullest, final, ultimate revelation of who God is.

---

* All Hebrews verse references being looked at in each chapter part are in **bold**.

The author makes his case by breaking down all of history into two parts. In the past God used to speak in certain ways; in the present, he speaks in a new way. For each of these, there are three things to notice. When did he speak? To whom did he speak? And how did he speak?

## God's Prior Way of Speaking

The first words in **verse 1** are "Long ago." From the very start, God has been a speaking God. In the very beginning, when God made the world, he did so by speaking (Genesis 1:3-27). By definition, God is a God who speaks.

So, it is not that when God speaks through Jesus, it is the first time he says something. No, he has been speaking for generations and generations. Who has he spoken to? To "our fathers." These are the generations of believers that have come before us. The author has Israel in mind primarily.

The most fundamental point, though, is *how* God spoke. "At many times and in many ways, God spoke ... by the prophets." That is, God used to speak through intermediaries. Not just anybody could speak for God: you had to be appointed as a prophet and inspired by God to speak for him. These chosen individuals were God's mouthpieces for speaking to his people.

The author is getting ready to tell us that Jesus is the full, final revelation of God and that God's new way of speaking is better than the old. But what he is *not* saying is that the old way is irrelevant or wrong. It is the inspired, infallible word of God. It is just incomplete—like a play without a final act. If you go to see a five-act play and it stops before the fifth act, you are disappointed: not because there was anything wrong with the first four acts but because the play hasn't finished yet. It needs an ending.

This is how we need to understand the author's view of the Old Testament. It is a single coherent story that ends on a cliffhanger: a story that needs an ending. God spoke to his people, and the cliffhanger is his promise to send a **redeemer** for them. When Jesus came, he resolved that cliffhanger.

So, the story of Jesus not a new story, but the finishing of an old one. The writer to the Hebrews is showing us that we need to look back at how God spoke at first, in order to understand how that led up to his final word in Jesus.

## God's New Way of Speaking

If you understand the overarching biblical story, Hebrews **1:2** is like the author lighting a piece of dynamite and throwing it into the room: "But in these last days, God has spoken to us by his Son."

For generations, the Israelites had been eagerly waiting and longing for the "last days"—that special time when God would intervene in the world and bring the redemption that he had promised. And now our author is saying that this has happened with the coming of Jesus. Finally, the story of the Bible has reached its climax. For the readers of the letter, this would have been a tremendous and exciting claim.

Of course, the phrase "last days" can be confusing. We tend to think it refers to a time in the future which will come right before Christ's second coming. But that's not how our author and the other New Testament authors use the phrase. For them, the "last days" are happening now! They began with Jesus' first coming and will last until his second coming.

Thus, the "last days" does not tell us about *how much* time we have left but about the *kind* of time we are in. To say we are in the "last days" means that we live in the world's last period of time (however long that lasts) before Jesus returns.

The language of this verse means that we live in a very privileged time. This should give us a sense of urgency. Our author is saying, *All those promises the Israelites have been waiting for over thousands of years, all those things you've been longing for God to do, have been completed in Christ. Now you're living in the last times.* God has spoken the final word in Christ, and it is time for us to respond. And so this is a time not to put our feet up but to spread the gospel faithfully.

God has, after all, spoken this word "to us." I love the personal nature of this. Do you ever feel as if God doesn't speak to you personally but only in a general sense, out there somewhere? The author of Hebrews is asserting that God has spoken to *you*. His word is for us today.

But the major difference between the way God spoke in the past and the way he speaks in the present is *how* he speaks. Here is the crescendo of **verses 1-2**. In the past, God used to speak through his intermediaries, but now he has shown up in person: "He has spoken to us by his Son." God came in the person of Christ, fully enfleshed, and spoke to his people himself. This is the stunning reality that makes the revelation of Jesus so special.

To help us to grasp this, our author next describes the glories of this Son. He shows his audience that Jesus is the fullest, final, most wonderful revelation of God himself.

## King: The Ultimate Ruler

These verses do several things to describe Jesus as the ultimate King. First (**v 2**), the author says that because Jesus is the Son, he is "appointed the heir of all things." That's what sons are—they are the heirs of all that belongs to their father. So the whole world, all of creation, belongs to Jesus; he is its King.

Jesus is also King in another way. Jesus is the one "through whom [God] created the world." He is the Creator (see also Colossians 1:16-17; John 1:3). This is a way of saying he is God—the ruler of the world—because creation is something that only God does.

A third thing to notice about Jesus' kingship is that "he upholds the universe by the word of his power" (Hebrews **1:3**). Again, this is a way to show that Jesus is God, because God is the One who sustains and upholds the world (see Psalm 104). Our author has taken attributes which are given to the God of Israel throughout the Old Testament and ascribed them to Jesus. He is the heir of the whole world, the one who sits on the throne as King; he is the Creator of the world, and the one who sustains it. Jesus is the Lord of the universe.

How would our lives look different if we thought about Jesus not just as our Savior from sin but also as the **sovereign** King of everything? How would focusing on Jesus as the ruler of all and master of the universe change our lives? We would be more prayerful. We would be less anxious because we would en-

> Jesus is not going to lose; he will prevail in the end, however dark things seem.

trust all our cares to Christ. (Of course, being fallen people, we would still worry; but this view of Jesus is the thing that will fight that.) And we'd be less despairing about the advance of the gospel, because we would remember that the great God who upholds the whole universe is the One leading his army forward. Jesus is not going to lose; the world is his inheritance, and he will prevail in the end, however dark things seem.

Let Jesus be your King. It will change your life.

## Prophet: The Ultimate Revealer of God

Next we see that Jesus is the ultimate prophet. If a prophet reveals God—his intentions, his character, his commands—then Jesus is better than any prophet who has ever gone before. This is because he is God enfleshed. Who can reveal God better than God?

This is clear in the language of Hebrews **1:3**: "He is the radiance of the glory of God." This word "radiance" means "brightness" or "shining." Old Testament visions of God describe him as bright and glorious (Exodus 24:10, 17; Ezekiel 1:4; Daniel 7:9). When Moses came down from Mount Sinai, his own face was shining because he had been speaking with God—shining so much that the people could not bear to come near him (Exodus 34:29-35). Likewise, during the time of the tabernacle, the glory of God would fill it, and the people would know he was there because of the brightness they could see (Exodus 40:34). Hebrews **1:3** says that all that glory, all that power, all that shining, is on Jesus.

In Jesus' earthly life this became evident at the Transfiguration (Matthew 17:1-8; Mark 9:2-8; Luke 9:28-36). Moses and Elijah, two key prophets, appeared and talked to Jesus; but they weren't being transfigured into glory. Only Jesus became a shining, bright white. When we read these accounts, we realize that Jesus is the way to come to God. He doesn't just reflect God's glory like Moses; he is himself the shining, bright, brilliant One.

Remember how Paul saw Jesus on the road: the light was so strong that he was blinded (Acts 9:3-8). Or think of the book of Revelation, in which John, one of Jesus' own disciples, meets Jesus afresh in his vision (Revelation 1:12-18). Jesus' glory is so stunning that John falls over like a dead man. This is the Jesus who is being described for us here. Jesus is the very glory of God.

He is, as Hebrews **1:3** continues, "the exact imprint of [God's] nature." Jesus perfectly represents God's being. The word "imprint" could also be translated "stamp" and was often used to describe the impression of an image on a coin. It referred to the exact image of the king or emperor. What the writer to the Hebrews is saying is that if you have seen Jesus, you have seen God. Jesus himself told us this: "Whoever has seen me has seen the Father" (John 14:9).

## Priest: The Ultimate Savior

Later in Hebrews we will unpack more fully what it meant to be a priest in the Old Testament, but for now it is enough to say that a priest made sacrifices for the sins of the people. The major difference with Jesus was that when he made sacrifices, he didn't offer bulls and goats. He offered himself.

This is described in the second half of Hebrews **1:3**. "After making purification for sins, he sat down at the right hand of the Majesty on high." Jesus has achieved what all of Israel had been longing for throughout generations: the real, full, final forgiveness of sins.

This is all the more amazing when we remember that Jesus is the ruler of the world and the exact imprint of God's nature. He is a king whom we have offended, against whom we often rebel; but he became a man and gave his own life for us. That's why it is important to understand all three roles or offices that Jesus has—king, prophet, and priest. If you think of Jesus just as a savior, you start taking him for granted. But if you realize that Jesus is also the King of the universe—if you realize that the King of the universe died for you and gave himself for you and laid aside everything for you—you are left thinking, "What king is this?" Kings don't save their enemies; they destroy them. Yet here is the Lord who has given himself in order to purify us from our sins.

And then "he sat down." In the Old Testament, while priests were doing their work, they never sat down. There was no chair inside the **tabernacle**. Their job was never done. Animal sacrifice doesn't take away sins, so the priests had to perform the rituals again and again and again. But Jesus paid for our sins and then sat down because his job was finished. The wrath of God is fully satisfied.

## Final Revelation

Have you ever read the Old Testament and thought to yourself, "I wish I could have seen what Moses saw," or "I wish I could have been a part of the life of Elijah"? In these first three verses of Hebrews, the writer's perspective is the opposite. In Jesus, God has given you a clearer, fuller revelation of himself than he gave to the Old Testament prophets. If only Moses had seen what you have seen!

We are living in the last days, when the fullness of the ages has come. We have seen God break into the world in the person of Jesus and rise from the dead to share his glory with the world. People were longing to see that for thousands of years; the angels long to look into it (1 Peter 1:10-12). But we are living in the "last days," when it has finally happened. The Old Testament days were not the glory days: they were days of shadows and types that only pointed toward Christ. But we have seen more than Moses ever imagined, because we are witnesses to the glory of Christ revealed on earth. This is the fundamental takeaway point from these verses: that we have the honor and privilege of living in the age of Christ, through whom God has fully and finally spoken.

## Questions for reflection

1. To what other places do you sometimes turn to hear God "speak" besides Jesus and the prophets?

2. What characteristics of Jesus stood out to you from this passage? How did those encourage you?

3. How should Jesus' position of power and exaltation affect your everyday life?

## PART TWO

Some people are really easy to impress. When my kids were growing up, they could have mac and cheese and chicken nuggets and think it was the greatest meal of all time. It just showed that there were a lot of culinary delights they had not experienced and didn't even know existed.

Most people are like that when it comes to where we seek satisfaction and fulfillment in life. We may think sex, drink, or financial gain is what life is all about. We may long for that perfect romantic relationship which will make life just the way we want it to be. These things impress us.

But the book of Hebrews tells us not to be so easily impressed by the things of the world. When we begin to see the Lord Jesus Christ in all his fullness, we realize that what we have been feeding on is like mac and cheese and chicken nuggets by comparison with him. Christ is more pleasing than anything else.

## Why the Concern over Angels?

In the context in which this letter was originally written, its Jewish audiences were also chasing around after other things, being more impressed by them than by Jesus. The thing that they were impressed by, however, was not job security or money or relationships; it was angels. This may seem irrelevant to us at first, but in fact it doesn't matter what the particular distraction is. The point is the same: don't be so easily impressed with the things of the world, because once you see Jesus in his glory, those things pale in comparison. He is superior to all things—angels included.

If you ever think about angels, you probably think of a sweet little creature who comes around and helps people from time to time. But in the Bible, angels are quite impressive. They are amazing, glorious creatures of God: his attendants and special servants. Every time an angel appears to somebody in the Bible, the first thing out of the angel's mouth is "Don't be afraid," because fear is the inevitable response to seeing them. An encounter with an angel is a glorious encounter, because angels reflect the glory of God.

In Isaiah 6:1-7, the prophet Isaiah has a vision of God on his throne, and part of this involves God's angelic attendants, the seraphim who fly around the throne. They are frightening creatures, zipping around with fire and lightning, wrapped with eyes all around (Revelation 4:8), which represents how God can see every single thing that is happening everywhere in the world at once. Angels are overwhelming and terrifying.

It seems as though the audience of this letter had begun to honor and venerate angels so that they took the place of Jesus for them. So the author unveils how great and glorious Christ is. He does this by walking through certain attributes of Jesus.

> The Old Testament doesn't just speak about Jesus; it is *all about* Jesus.

The writer's methodology for proving the superiority of Jesus over angels is to use Scripture: specifically, the Old Testament. This is because Jesus is the God of the Old Testament. The Old Testament doesn't just speak about Jesus; it is *all about* Jesus (Luke 24:27).

We may need to recalibrate the way we think about the Old Testament. We know that it was incomplete and that a fuller, final revelation was necessary. At the same time, we must remember that the Old Testament is absolutely true and authoritative and speaks of Jesus. Our author demonstrates this by his methodology here.

He gives us seven Old Testament passages. The number seven is noteworthy because it is a sign of completion in the Bible. But we can divide them up into four points: four attributes of Jesus. Jesus has a better name than the angels; he is worshiped by angels; he rules the angels; and he made the angels.

Are the angels glorious? Of course. Are they impressive? On one level, yes. But when you look at Christ in all his glory and wonder and beauty and magnificence, you realize you've been chasing the wrong thing. As we read these verses, we will be renewed again in our apprehension of the glory and greatness of Christ.

## A Better Name

First, in Hebrews **1:4-5**, Jesus has a name that is "more excellent" than the names of the angels. Remember that this name is the Son of God: the name above all names. We saw in verses 2-3 that to be the Son means to be the heir of the world and to share in the glory and divinity of the Father. Our author knows that Jesus has a status that no angel could even come close to competing with. In **verse 5** he pulls out two **proof texts**.

The first is Psalm 2:7: "You are my Son, today I have begotten you." The second is a quote from 2 Samuel 7:14: "I will be to him a father, and he shall be to me a son."

When you first read these passages, it may seem as though there was a time when Jesus was not the Son, and then a point when he became the Son. How could that be? That makes it sound as though Jesus is lesser than God, or that he came into existence at some point. But the Bible affirms that Jesus has *always* existed, throughout eternity (John 1:1-2).

Similarly, when we hear the word "Son," we may be tempted to think that means that Jesus is secondary or inferior to the Father. Nothing could be further from the truth. The Son shares in the same eternal, divine nature as the Father.

Therefore, these passages likely have in view the moment when Jesus was "declared to be the Son of God in power" (Romans 1:4; see also Acts 13:33). This moment was his resurrection, which was his great inauguration—his ascending to his place of honor and glory.

This is something the Roman world would have understood. When sons came of age, they were formally bestowed with the family name, even though in one sense they had always had it. My own son, John, has my name and is my son; there's nothing that can change that. But if we were living in the Roman world, when John came of age he would be bestowed with and credited with the family name in a formal way. He would "become" my son. This is the best way to understand Jesus' sonship status. He "came of age" when he ascended into glory. This is why Psalm 2:7 can say that "today," namely on the day of resurrection, Jesus was appointed as the Son (see also 2 Samuel 7:14).

And no angel ever had this status as the heir of the universe, the very Son of God.

## Worshiped by Angels

In Hebrews **1:6**, we come to a second attribute of Jesus: he is worshiped by angels.

Besides being afraid, one thing that people in the Bible do when they meet angels is to try to worship them. They are so overwhelmed with the glory of the angel that they bow down. We see this in Revelation 19:10 in particular, where John—even the apostle John—tries to worship an angel. But the response from the angel is *No, no, no. There's only one person to worship, and I'm not him.*

In Isaiah 6 the angels who are so terrifying as they fly around the throne of God are actually worshiping God (v 3). In fact, they are so overwhelmed by the glory of God that they have two extra pairs of wings specifically for covering themselves so that they are shielded from the glory of God (v 2). If a sinless being like an angel cannot even look at the glory of God, what does that say about sinful beings like you and me?

John 12:41 alludes to that passage, telling us that the One who was lifted up on that throne is in fact Jesus. The Glorious Almighty—the magnificent, overwhelming, shining One at whom the angels cannot even bear to look, and of whom they spend all their time singing—is Jesus. People may find angels mesmerizing, but angels themselves are mesmerized by Jesus.

In Hebrews 1 the author's point can't be missed: *You're impressed by angels, are you? Tempted perhaps even to worship them, are you? But do you realize how impressed angels are with Christ? They are absolutely blown away by his glory.* Angels are like a Junior Varsity team: they may seem impressive but they're not playing major league. Jesus is.

We can learn from the angels the way to understand and recognize the superiority of Jesus: we should worship him. Come to church to be reminded of who he is, to be confronted with the glory of the Lord of the universe, and to be helped to go back to following him. Worship is essential for reminding us why Jesus is better. We are fellow servants with the angels (Revelation 19:10) and should follow their example; the whole theme of our lives should be to give glory to God and to worship Christ.

## Ruler of the Angels

In Hebrews **1:8-9** the author cites Psalm 45. Notice the throne language: it's about kingship. But also notice the way Hebrews **1:8** is set up. Speaking of the Son, "he" (God) says, "Your throne, O God." When we read about God on his throne in the Old Testament, we should see that as applying to Christ.

We see this, too, in **verse 13**, which cites Psalm 110. "To which of the angels has he ever said, 'Sit at my right hand until I make your enemies a footstool for your feet'?" The phrase "the right hand of God" is found all through the Bible. This is not a subordinate position, as though Jesus were a junior God. No, to be at the right hand of God is to be the One who has all God's authority and all his sovereign rule. It's a position of power. In fact, to be at the right hand of God is eventually to be the person who will come to conquer and judge the world.

Notice the language here: his enemies will be "a footstool for [his] feet." Jesus is not just a king but a warrior king—the One who will destroy all his enemies and set all things right.

Hebrews **1:7** contains another quote from the Old Testament, in which the author shows that the angels are Jesus' servants or "ministers." He says the same thing in **verse 14**: "Are they not all ministering spirits sent out to serve for the sake of those who are to inherit salvation?" In other words, angels serve Jesus. They do his bidding because he is the King.

The implications of this are monumental. First, if you realize that the King of the universe is your friend—that he sends ministering spirits out to serve for your sake—then you know you have someone to turn to for whatever help you need in times of trouble.

Second, if Jesus is the great King who will vanquish his foes, every person in the world needs to ask the question, "Am I on the Lord's side?" Do we really want to fight against this King? It's a sobering point. *Those glorious angels you're so impressed with, they cower before this King,* the author is saying, *and yet you defy him. Do you really want to do that?*

This is not just a call to unbelievers, telling them that if they are not on the Lord's side, they are in danger. It is a call to believers, saying that if you know you are living some part of your life in disobedience, you need to repent and come back to the King.

## Creator of the Angels

The final trump card that the writer plays is the fact that Jesus made the angels. He created everything, and that includes them. We see this in **verses 10-12**, where Psalm 102 is cited: "You, Lord, laid the foundation of the earth in the beginning, and the heavens are the work of your hands." Our author sees this psalm text about creation and asserts that God is talking there about Jesus.

The implication is that he is eternal. He does not wear out like the world (Hebrews **1:11**). He is forever and ever.

As we pull these four attributes of Christ together across these seven quotations, we are reminded of the major theme of the book of Hebrews: how glorious Jesus is. We must be impressed not with the things of the world that we're chasing but with Christ. Instead of being easily pleased with angels, or with whatever fills that slot for us—sex, money, power, or anything else—we must look to the glory of Christ. He is the One who has a name above all other names, who is the only person worthy of worship, who rules all things and who is the One by whom all things were made. It is Christ alone who should captivate our hearts.

## Questions for reflection

1. Are you too easily impressed with things other than Jesus? What are some of those things, and how does this passage help you correct your thinking about them?

2. How can Jesus' identity as the King of the universe help you work through the challenges in your life today? How might this change your worship?

3. What else especially strikes you about Jesus' identity in this passage? Will you speak about him differently as a result of reading Hebrews 1?

# 2. A GREAT SALVATION

## We Tend to Drift

Have you ever been out on the ocean in a boat? Unlike on a lake, if you turn the motor off and just sit there floating, you don't stay in one spot: you drift in the current. You look up to find you are somewhere completely different. Without doing anything at all, you have drifted away.

It is the same in the Christian life. Drifting happens very easily and imperceptibly. For this reason, our author says, "we must pay much closer attention to what we have heard, *lest we drift away from it*" (**2:1**).

Here is something that we rarely want to admit: there is a part of each of us that tends to be drawn to things other than Jesus. Left to themselves, our hearts tend to drift away from God.

Many things can lead us to drift. It could be suffering, which derails our faith; or opposition, which makes us want to give up; or busyness, which distracts us from our spiritual life. It could be holding on to sin instead of repenting. These things can draw us away from God.

It can even be little things that cause us to drift away. C.S. Lewis illustrates this in his book *The Screwtape Letters*, in which one demon gives advice to another:

> "The safest road to Hell is the gradual one—the gentle slope,
> soft underfoot without sudden turnings, without milestones,
> without signposts." (p 56)

Now, to be clear, someone who is truly saved, who is truly a Christian, cannot ultimately lose their salvation—although they may have periods of disobedience or **backsliding**. However, we are given this warning to spur us on and to make us examine ourselves. There is a danger that we may think we are believers but end up proving by our estrangement from Jesus that we never really knew God.

This warning is for each one of us. At the Last Supper, when Jesus said, "One of you will betray me," the disciples did not respond by saying, *Well, we all know it's going to be Judas!* No, they said, *Surely not I, Rabbi?* (Matthew 26:21-25). They wondered, *Is it me?* They took the warning seriously for themselves. We too need to ask ourselves, "Could it be me? Could I drift away?"

## God Holds People Accountable

Our author isn't finished. He provides a second reason to pay attention to the message of the gospel: God holds us accountable for our response to it.

Indeed, God held his people accountable even during the time of the Old Testament. Hebrews **2:2** reminds us that "every **transgression** or disobedience [under the old covenant] received a just retribution." When the Israelites disobeyed the message of salvation—when they rejected him and refused to receive his grace—he held them accountable (e.g. Exodus 32:35; Leviticus 10:1-3; Numbers 11:33; 14:20-23; Joshua 7:1-26).

We sometimes think that that Old Testament God is different from the God we read about in the New Testament. We think that the old covenant is all about **wrath** and judgment, and the new covenant is all about love and grace. But Hebrews **2:3** shows us that this is not true: "How shall we escape if we neglect such a great salvation?" The point is that if we reject the message of Jesus, we too will be held accountable.

Not only this, but we are even more culpable for rejecting Jesus' message than people were for rejecting the old covenant. The author contrasts the "message declared by angels," which revealed God in types and shadows, with the "great salvation" of Jesus, in whom God's glory was fully displayed. If God was upset when the prophets were rejected, how much more do you think he will be upset if the Son is rejected?

At the same time, of course, we can see God's great mercy in **verse 3**. The message that we must not neglect is the "great salvation" of Jesus Christ. We can escape the justice of God by embracing Jesus, who offered himself as the solution to our problem of sin. He has made a way of escape for us. We must pay attention to the message of Jesus because it provides the way out from God's judgment.

## The Message Is Clear and True

In **verses 3-4**, we see a third reason to pay attention: namely that this message of salvation is absolutely clear, trustworthy, and reliable.

First, the author says that this message "was declared at first by the Lord" (**v 3**). It did not come through an intermediary as the old covenant did. God, enfleshed in Jesus, came himself and spoke. This means that we have no need to worry about distortion in the message.

He goes on to say that "it was attested to us by those who heard." This is a reference to the apostles, the eyewitnesses of Jesus' teachings, death, and resurrection. *This is not something I made up,* says our author. *There are eyewitnesses whom you and I know and have heard from.*

The message was also confirmed by the Spirit. Look at **verse 4**: "God also bore witness by signs and wonders and various miracles." The message of salvation was authenticated by the amazing miracles performed by Jesus, capped off by his resurrection.

The final reason for knowing that the message is true is because of the "gifts of the Holy Spirit distributed according to his will." God has gifted each and every Christian in some special way that allows us to bless **the body of Christ** and the world around us. One of the things that reassures us most in our faith is when we see the Spirit at work in God's people around us. It gives us confidence that the gospel message is true.

We need to wake up and make sure we are proactively listening to this message, because it is clear, trustworthy, and reliable. We will be held accountable by our just God if we neglect it by drifting away. But we are all too likely to drift away if we don't pay attention. That is the first warning in the book of Hebrews.

## God's Plan for Humanity

In **verse 5** the author begins to tell us more about this message. He is going to explain how God became a man to save human beings. Jesus is the ultimate human—the perfect human—who is able to represent us before God.

To do this, the author first shifts the focus to us as humans: who we are and what we were made to be and do.

When it comes to the question of what it means to be human, people usually shoot either too high or too low. Some think of humans as little gods: everything is measured by what we think and what we want and what we do. Others say that there is nothing significant or unique or special about humans at all; we are nothing but little dust mites in a big universe.

Many people hold on to both these extremes at the same time without even realizing it. On the one hand they talk about how humanity is insignificant in the universe, and on the other hand they treat humans as if they are the measure of all things.

But this passage rejects both these views. It tells us that humans have glory and dignity and honor because we are made in the image of God. At the same time, we are not God. We are not the measure of all things. We have messed up the world and need to be redeemed.

In **verse 5**, the author indicates that "it was not to angels that God subjected the world to come." In other words, humans stand out in creation: we are greater than angels. One day we are going to rule the world.

But why is that the case? In **verses 6-8** he quotes from Psalm 8. This psalm begins by reflecting on how small humanity seems in the world, registering surprise that God would notice us: "What is man, that you are mindful of him, or the son of man, that you care for him?"

Yet God has made us for a special purpose. In **verse 7** we see two things that God has made us for. First, we're to reflect God's glory. "You have crowned him"—that is humanity, mankind, you and me— "with glory and honor." This is an echo of Genesis 1:26, where we are told that we are made in God's image. We reflect something about him that no other created being does. Each one of us is a little reflection of him. That is why he wants us to "be fruitful and multiply and fill the earth" (Genesis 1:28): because the more human beings there are, the more God's image and glory are spread.

Hebrews **2:8** reminds us that we are also designed to rule God's world. It describes God "putting everything in subjection under [man's] feet." God made human beings to be the guardians, protectors, and rulers of his world. He intended it that way for his glory and our blessing.

This is why angels are not given dominion over the world. Here is a stunning verse—1 Corinthians 6:3: "Do you not know that we are to judge angels?" We tend to think of angels as more glorious than us—and at the moment, as Hebrews **2:7a** tells us, humans are indeed "for a little while lower" than them—but someday we will have a role in ruling and judging them.

> God made human beings to be the guardians, protectors, and rulers of his world.

We need to recognize this distinctive glory and dignity of humans. Every person you run into is a little immortal, made in the image of God. Every person—poor or wealthy, notorious sinner or respected member of the community—should be shown dignity and honor. Humans have a distinctive purpose: to reflect God's glory and rule his world.

## What Happened?

But things didn't go that way. In **verse 8** we see that God designed everything to be under the dominion of his vice-regents, the human beings he created. However, "at present, we do not yet see everything in subjection to him [mankind]."

The truth is that we are not ruling the world well, and we are not reflecting God's glory well. We have messed up the idea of ruling so badly that when we think of the word "ruler," we often think of someone who lords it over others—someone who oppresses. That was not God's intention for rulers. But we've blown it. And so, the world is a profoundly broken place.

There is a rich irony in God's plan for humanity. We were designed to rule over angels, and yet it was an angelic being (Satan) who persuaded Adam and Eve to follow him and rebel against God. Instead of judging and ruling over angels, the first humans subjected themselves to angels. Instead of rebuking Satan, they listened to him. The ultimate result was that God's design for the world was profoundly broken.

People will tell you that the problem with the world is lack of education, or bad cultural influences, or economic inequality; if those things were sorted out, the world would be a better place. But in all those scenarios, the problem is still there as long as we are still there. It is not just that Adam sinned; his corruption has passed down to all humans after him. *In short, you and I are the problem with the world.* And if we're the problem, we can't be the solution. Education, government programs, and cultural change are not enough, because they are human solutions. No, we can't save ourselves.

So how *can* human beings be restored to the glory and honor that God intended? We need a perfect human to represent us. We need someone who can take our place and succeed where we failed. Sure enough, in verse 9, the author will begin to apply this psalm text not to humanity in general but to one human in particular—Jesus.

## Questions for reflection

1. What are some steps you might need to take to keep yourself from drifting away and missing the message of salvation in Jesus?

2. Do you have a tendency to think that God is just and holy in the Old Testament, but not in the New? How does this passage correct that misconception?

3. How does the reminder of the value of human beings help reshape the goals of your life and ministry?

## PART TWO

Have you ever had a conversation with someone in which you tried to convince them that Jesus was God? That happens a lot in our world. But when was the last time you had a conversation with someone and you had to convince them Jesus was really *human*? Probably never! People just take it for granted that Jesus was really a man.

But this wasn't the case in the ancient world. There were a number of groups—particularly the **Gnostics**—who struggled to believe that Jesus could really be a human like us. For them, since Jesus was divine, there was no way he could take on the limitations of the flesh.

So our author now wants to show that the glorious King of the universe humbled himself and became a real human being, "made lower than the angels" (**verse 9**). He is both God and man. And because Christ is the perfect human being, he can deliver us from the problem we have got ourselves into. By becoming human, he was able to "taste death for everyone."

**Verse 10** tells us that Jesus was made "perfect through suffering." This doesn't refer to the moral perfection of Jesus—he was always sinless—but to his effectiveness as our representative. By suffering as a man, he became a more sympathetic, more appropriate, more fitting high priest for us.

Here is where we see how our salvation depends as much on Jesus' humanity as it does on his divinity. If he was not really human, then he could not really represent us. And if he could not represent us, he could not save us.

## Jesus Brings Salvation

Since Jesus is our perfect human representative, that allows him to be the "founder" of our salvation (**v 10**). Think of Jesus as a "pioneer," carving a path forward so that we can follow in his footsteps. This means that if you trust in Jesus, what is true of him is true of you.

There are three aspects of this union with Christ to pull out from **verses 9-13**.

First, Jesus' death is our death. Jesus was crowned with glory "because of the suffering of death, so that by the grace of God he might taste death for everyone" (**v 9**).

Sinners deserve to die, and yet in Christ we are saved because he died in our place. This is why Paul says that he has "been crucified with Christ" (Galatians 2:20; see also Romans 6:1-10). The penalty Paul deserved to pay has been paid by Jesus on his behalf, and now Paul is living a new life. It is the same for us. Christ has died our death.

Second, Jesus' glory is our glory. When Jesus was raised from the dead, he was "crowned with glory and honor" (Hebrews **2:9**). That is the future that awaits us too. He brings "many sons to glory" (**v 10**). Because Jesus has paid the penalty for our sin, we will be raised up to the place of dignity that God always intended for us.

Third, Jesus' holiness is our holiness. **Verse 11** tells us that he "**sanctifies**" and we "are sanctified." This holiness makes us part of the same family—God's family—so that Jesus can call us "brothers" (**v 12**, citing Psalm 22:22) and "the children God has given me" (Hebrews **2:13**, citing Isaiah 8:18).

Think of Jesus' temptation in the wilderness. That was the first time in the history of the world that Satan tempted a human and the human never sinned. Adam sinned; Abraham sinned; Moses sinned; Joshua sinned. Every single human who ever walked the earth sinned. But along came Jesus, enduring 40 days in the desert, hungry and suffering, and he succeeded where every other human had failed. For the first time ever, Satan was defeated.

This is the holiness that is credited to us if we trust in Jesus. When God looks on us, he sees the perfect righteous obedience of his Son.

Jesus died our death, gives us his holiness, and will lead us to glory. In Christ, God promises to make us into the kind of humanity he originally designed. This was always his plan.

## An Effective High Priest

In the next verses the author shows us how it is that Jesus was able to do all these things. He is a great high priest who represents us perfectly to God.

In a court of law, we all know that it is unwise to represent yourself. You need someone who understands the way the system works and how to make your case effectively: someone to represent you well to the judge. And it is the same in God's courtroom. If we try to stand before God on our own merits, making our own arguments, and using our own ability, the verdict will always be guilty.

> This is like the lawyer who represents you actually going to prison on your behalf.

In ancient Israel there was someone whose job it was to represent Israel before God: the high priest. Every year this man would enter into the holiest part of the temple to make certain sacrifices on behalf of the people.

There were two problems with this system. The first problem was that the sacrifices kept having to be made, year after year. The blood of animals didn't really take away sins. The second problem was that the high priests came and went: one would die and another would be appointed, and then that one would die. Some of these priests would be good at their job, and some would be bad. The men who filled the office of high priest were unreliable.

A better kind of high priest was needed: someone who would represent us to God more effectively.

Of course, we know who that is: Jesus Christ.

This is explained further in Hebrews **2:14-18**, where we see two aspects of Jesus' humanity that make him an effective high priest for us. First, he is a real human, which means he can represent humans and make a perfect sacrifice for us. Second, he really has experienced the life of a human, which means he can understand us and perfectly **intercede** for us.

## Real Humanity

Look at **verse 14**: "Since therefore the children share in flesh and blood, he himself likewise partook of the same things." This is very raw language. It doesn't just say that Jesus had a body or that he was a man: it says he took on "flesh and blood." Jesus is a real human in every way. This is a core **theological** truth. Jesus had to become a human in order to represent humans.

This is explained in **verse 16**. Did Jesus set out on a plan to save angels? No. He set out on a plan to save you and me—"the offspring of Abraham." Jesus became flesh and blood because he is out to help flesh and blood. He became a human so that he could die as a human, for us.

This kind of high priest was not what a first-century Jew would have expected. The ancient priests offered sacrifices, but Jesus offered himself. He became both priest and sacrifice. This is like the lawyer who represents you in the lawcourt actually going to prison on your behalf.

Jesus' death accomplishes two things which make his sacrifice more effective than any sacrifice offered before. First, his death defeats the devil. Second, his death satisfies God's wrath.

Look at **verses 14-15**. The reason Jesus took on flesh and blood was "that through death he might destroy the one who has the power of death, that is, the devil, and deliver all those who through fear of death were subject to lifelong slavery."

When we say that Satan "has the power of death," it is not to say that he has the ultimate power and that he really controls the power of death. We know that God is the One who gives life and takes it away (1 Samuel 2:6). No, Satan has the power of death in the sense that he influences the thing that causes death.

Death is the result of rebellion against God. It is the penalty for sin. This means that the only way to defeat death is to defeat sin. To try to deal with the penalty without dealing with the cause would be of no use at all. That's why Jesus died: to bear sin (Isaiah 53:12; Hebrews 9:28; 1 Peter 2:24). By his death he defeated the devil and the power of death (Hebrews **2:14**; 1 Corinthians 15:20-26).

This means that death is no longer a threat. We will all die physically, but death doesn't master us, because we will live again in Christ.

Notice the way Hebrews **2:15** puts it: he died to "deliver all those who through fear of death were subject to lifelong slavery." Jesus' death sets us free not only from sin but also from the fear of death. This should radically change our lives. You can really live for Christ if you know that death has no power over you.

I'm not suggesting we should go out and risk our lives recklessly, but we do need to think about how much the fear of death holds us. We spend so much time thinking about how long we are going to live and planning for the time we have left. But in Christ we live eternally. We need to get the fear of death off our shoulders and live like we are going to live forever.

The second thing that Jesus' death did was to satisfy the wrath of God. **Verse 17** says that he became a high priest "to make propitiation for the sins of the people."

"Propitiation" is a specific word which means that Jesus' death satisfies God's wrath against sin—it appeases God. Jesus is like a sponge which soaks up all the wrath of God so that there is no more left. At the cross he was cursed with the curse we deserve (Galatians 3:13).

God is right to be angry at sin, but do you need to fear that anger? No. If you trust in Jesus, there is no anger left for you. It has been totally satisfied by Jesus' death. God's favor now rests on you, and you do not need to be afraid.

Jesus is a real human being who died a real death, and this means he has accomplished all that for you. He has defeated sin—the power of death—and therefore defeated Satan. And he has satisfied the wrath of God. Now we can live a life without fear.

## Real Suffering

But there is more to be said. The point is not just that Jesus was a real human being; it is that he also experienced the life of a real human being. If all Jesus had to do was to become a real human and then die for our sins, then between birth and death he could have hidden out in a castle somewhere, living a life of protection—a perfect, solitary existence. But in fact, he lived the life of a human being. He experienced the very worst of what you and I experience.

Nobody ever looked at Jesus' life and said, "I wish I had a life like that." He had a brutally hard existence. This is critical to understanding why he is such an effective high priest: because he can relate to you and me.

Jesus experienced everything we experience. That's in **verse 17**: "He had to be made like his brothers in every respect." **Verse 18** tells us what this means: "he himself has suffered when tempted." Suffering and temptation are the things that mark Jesus' human experience.

Ever felt abandoned or lonely? Jesus can relate: he is the "man of sorrows" (Isaiah 53:3), rejected and put to death by his own people. Ever felt the grief of losing someone you love? Jesus can relate: he wept at the death of Lazarus (John 11:35). Ever been lied about? Jesus can relate: he was betrayed by a close friend, falsely accused by the priests, and ridiculed by the soldiers. Ever had money problems? Jesus was poor and had "nowhere to lay his head" (Matthew 8:20). Ever felt misunderstood by a family member? Jesus' own family thought he had lost his mind (Mark 3:21). Ever felt highly stressed? Jesus was so stressed in the Garden of Gethsemane that his sweat was like drops of blood (Luke 22:44).

No one could ever go to Jesus and say, "You don't understand my life." It's us who cannot understand how much *he* suffered in *his* life.

Jesus was also tempted in all the ways we are tempted. The temptation of personal glory: *Throw yourself off this temple, Jesus, and the angels will lift you up* (Luke 4:9-12). The temptation of wealth and power: *I'll give you all the nations if you'll just bow down and worship me* (Luke 4:5-8). Perhaps the greatest temptation Jesus experienced was in the Garden of Gethsemane, when he said, "Take this cup from me" (Luke 22:42). He was tempted to do anything he could to avoid suffering.

Jesus never gave in to temptation, but that doesn't mean he did not feel it. It means he felt it even more. We get a reprieve from temptation because we give in to it; if we did not give in, it would build and mount and grow. Can you imagine going through life with all those temptations hanging over you, with no reprieve, and never giving in even once? Jesus absolutely understands what it is like to be tempted.

Jesus' suffering matters because it means that Jesus could take on two characteristics as high priest: he could be *merciful* and *faithful* (Hebrews **2:17**).

The problem with the ordinary high priest in ancient Judaism was not only that sacrifices had to be made again and again but also that the priest himself was unreliable. Each one would die. What was needed was someone who would never give up and never go away: someone faithful.

Jesus is that faithful high priest. He intercedes for you and will always do so, every moment of your life. He never calls in sick. The evidence for this is the fact that he suffered and was tempted. If he endured all that faithfully, then he will also be faithful as a high priest: always there for you, always praying for you, always acting as your good representative before God.

Suffering also made him a merciful high priest. Jesus is compassionate toward us because he knows what it is like to be in any difficult situation we might find ourselves in.

We know from our own experiences that suffering can make us more compassionate and merciful. It is one of God's greatest tools to shape us. When we suffer, we should think, "God may be preparing me for some special ministry through this." He may be preparing you to be merciful to people in your own life. He uses suffering for good.

Likewise, he used it for good in Jesus' life—for *our* good. Jesus suffered and was tempted, and that made him "able to help those who are being tempted" (**v 18**).

Jesus is fully divine and fully human, our perfect representative before God, who offered himself to bring us to glory. He is better than any other high priest anyone could possibly imagine.

## Questions for reflection

1. How does the fear of death affect your life? In what ways does the truth of this passage allow you to live a more daring life for Christ?

2. What are some of the struggles you are facing today, and how does Jesus' own experience of those same sorts of struggles encourage you?

3. How are you doing in showing sympathy and compassion to others? How does this passage help you?

# 3. LOOK AND LISTEN

## Fix Your Eyes on Jesus

On August 7, 1974, a Frenchman named Philippe Petit did something remarkable. In the middle of the night he stretched a cable between the two towers of the World Trade Center in downtown Manhattan (which were still under construction). Early the next morning, with awestruck crowds watching below, Petit walked back and forth across the cable multiple times, performing one of the world's most daring high-wire acts.

When we behold a feat like this, we have one simple question: how did he keep from falling? For high-wire performers, there is one simple answer. You keep your eyes focused on the destination and never look down.

Hebrews **3:1** tells us that it works that way in the Christian life. If we are to keep from falling, we need to "consider Jesus." I prefer the way the NIV translates it: "Fix your eyes on Jesus." Don't look down, but stay focused on him.

Peter learned this lesson the hard way. In Matthew 14:22-33 the disciples are out on the Sea of Galilee in a boat, and they see Jesus walking toward them across the water. When they realize who it is, Peter gets out of the boat and walks on the water toward Jesus.

While Peter is looking at Jesus, all is well. But when he focuses on the wind and the waves, he starts to sink.

You and I, like Peter, are very easily distracted from Jesus. We fix our eyes on just about anything sometimes. We all have a tendency in our heart to follow other gods, as it were, which we think might satisfy us more than Jesus. That's what the original recipients of this letter were doing—thinking maybe they should go back to Judaism. The author is saying to them and to us, *No! Don't get distracted, or you'll start to sink.*

Hebrews **3:1-6** gives us two reasons to fix our eyes on Jesus.

## Who You Are

The first part of **verse 1** directly addresses and identifies the audience. When the author does this, he is identifying you and me too, because this letter is written to all of Christ's people. He addresses us as "holy brothers ... who share in a heavenly calling."

Before we get to the command to consider Jesus, we need to start where the passage starts: with understanding how God sees us. The author takes us through three things which tend to form identity, showing us who we are in Christ.

First, he calls us holy. He doesn't just say, *Therefore, brothers*; he says, "Therefore, holy brothers." He calls you holy; he calls me holy; and he calls the audience he is writing to holy.

You might think this is strange. Does he not know his audience? Does he not realize that his audience is filled with sinners? Is he naïve, unaware, or just simplistic here? Alternatively, you might think, "He clearly isn't talking about me." He is talking about holy people, but you know your own heart, and you are definitely not holy.

But here is the truth: in this one word, we see that a radical identity transformation has taken place for Christians. God regards us as holy. That doesn't mean that Christians are perfect, that we have got our act together, or that we do not still struggle with sin. But it does mean that there is something different about us. We belong to Christ, we have the Spirit in us, and we have been set apart for God's purposes.

Realizing that you are holy makes you see sin for the big deal that it is. Too often we say, "Well, I'm only human," letting ourselves off the hook. But if you identify yourself as holy, then you see sin as something that is entirely against who you are.

That would make you miserable were it not for the fact that being holy also gives you hope. God has set you on a new trajectory. By his Spirit, you are set apart for his purposes. He is at work in you.

Second, our identity also involves a new family. He calls us "brothers." This of course includes both brothers and sisters. The idea is very simple: you don't belong to these other things, because you have a new family in Christ. Jesus is your brother (2:11).

All through my teenage years, whenever I did something wrong, my father would say, "That is not what Krugers do." He wanted me to act in accordance with my family identity. Likewise, understanding that we are part of the family of God is an incredibly important way of keeping us on track in our faith.

> You belong with Jesus. That is who you are.

This highlights the significance of church. Christians gather in groups because being together matters. The word is taught in community; church is an incredibly powerful tool that God uses to remind you that you belong in his family.

Third, we also have a new citizenship. He calls his audience "you who share in a heavenly calling." We are called toward a heavenly destination: we will dwell with God forever in the new heavens and the new earth. That is our homeland; that is our country.

Who you are as a citizen is part of your identity. The values that your country stands for influence you. You are proud of where you come from and you seek to represent your country well. It is the same thing here. You belong with Jesus; he has called you to his country. That is who you are. Therefore, fix your eyes on him.

## Who Jesus Is

"Consider Jesus" is the very next phrase in **3:1**. What are we to consider about Jesus? First, he is the bridge between us and God.

The author gives Jesus two titles: he calls him "the apostle and high priest of our confession." These two terms are not accidentally linked together. They work as a summary of much of what has been discussed in the first two chapters of the letter.

"Apostle" means "sent." As you read the term "apostle," you are likely to think about the twelve apostles whom Jesus sent out. But in fact, Jesus himself was the very first apostle. In John 20:21, Jesus says, "As the Father has sent me, even so I am sending you." He was an apostle before his disciples were. Jesus was sent by God to speak for God to humans (Hebrews 1:2)—which is what an apostle does.

A high priest goes in the opposite direction. He represents humans to God, bringing offerings into the temple on their behalf. We saw this in 2:17-18.

Jesus, uniquely, is both an apostle and a priest. He goes *both ways*. He can do this because he is both God and man. Who better to represent God to humans than God? Who better to represent humans to God than a human? Jesus alone is both these things. That is why I use the term "bridge." Jesus perfectly bridges the gap between humans and God.

## Greater Than Moses

If you were a first-century Jew it would be hard to find a figure who ranked higher in your mind than Moses. Moses led the Israelites out of Egypt in the **exodus**, a crucial and foundational moment in the story of God's people. Moses was the one who delivered **the law** and set up the whole system of temple worship. He is also the author of the first five books of the Bible. He is a major pillar of the Jewish faith.

Yet Jesus is so much more glorious than Moses. This is the argument which our author now develops in **3:2-6**.

He starts by praising both Jesus and Moses. Look at **verse 2**: Jesus "was faithful to [God] … just as Moses also was faithful in all God's house." Both are faithful servants of God, to be praised and honored.

Our author will not disparage Moses. He does not say that Moses was wrong and that we are thankful to Jesus for fixing his mistakes. No, Jesus doesn't fix or correct Moses. He fulfills all that Moses pointed toward.

In the following verses there are two big differences between Moses and Jesus. Moses is in the house as part of God's people, but Jesus is over the house. And Moses is described as a servant of God's house, but Jesus is God's Son. They are on the same team, but Jesus surpasses Moses.

The shift happens in **verse 3**. "For Jesus has been counted worthy of more glory than Moses—as much more glory as the builder of a house has more honor than the house itself." Moses was only part of the house, while Christ built the house.

Look forward to **verse 6**: "And we are [God's] house." This is a remarkable statement. The average Jewish reader might have assumed the author is talking about a physical building—the Old Testament temple. But the house that God is building through Jesus Christ is not a physical structure; it is the *people of God*. The community of believers is God's real "house." Indeed, elsewhere Peter refers to Christians as "living stones [which] are being built up as a spiritual house" (1 Peter 2:5).

In short, Moses was part of the people of God, whereas Jesus is the *creator* and *builder* of the people of God. Why is Jesus able to do this? Because he is God. Hebrews **3:4**: "For every house is built by someone, but the builder of all things is God." Moses pointed toward the coming Savior—he came "to testify to the things that were to be spoken later" (**v 5**)—but Jesus is the Savior himself.

In **verses 5-6** the house imagery is used in a different way. "Now Moses was faithful in all God's house as a servant ... but Christ is faithful over God's house as a son."

Imagine you are paying a house call to someone very wealthy who lives on a big estate. You are met at the door by a servant, who greets you and brings you in. But this servant is not the owner of the house.

He is not the one you are there to see. The servant may do his job well, but you are there to see the son—the heir to the estate. He is the one whom you honor.

In the same way, although Moses and Jesus are both faithful, it is Jesus who is most worthy of honor. He is the builder of the house. He is the Son of God.

Let me draw out a couple of implications.

First, notice that there is only one house. The author is not contrasting Moses' house with Jesus' house. It is all one house. There is a single people of God throughout all the history of the world. Moses was the shepherd of those people in the Old Testament, and we call them Israel; yet he was only pointing toward the coming of Jesus, who would continue that same people of God in the church. Israel and the church are not two separate peoples of God. There is one people of God: the church is the continuation of Israel.

This means that we must not think of the Old Testament as completely irrelevant to us. It is not. In Christ we become heirs of the promises which were made to Abraham and his descendants through **Isaac** (Galatians 3:29). So we need to pay attention to those promises and stories.

The second implication stems from the fact that as followers of Jesus we are God's house. Ephesians 2:19-22 sheds light on this:

"You are fellow citizens with the saints and members of the household of God ... Christ Jesus himself being the **cornerstone**, in whom the whole structure, being joined together, grows into a holy temple in the Lord. In him you are also being built together into a dwelling place for God by the Spirit."

In the church, Christ dwells. After all, we are his house. Not only does he live in individual Christians by the power of the Holy Spirit but we are all "being built together into a dwelling place for God." The Spirit of Christ lives in his corporate body, the church.

In our world today, the spirit of individualism reigns supreme. It is tempting to think, "I don't need a church. I'll just show up when I feel like it. I might hop around, do a little church shopping, figure out what I like, and if I don't like it, move on." That is the spirit of the age. But that is not the spirit we see in the book of Hebrews. You are the people of God, and God dwells in your midst. That means it is vital to be committed to one another and linked together as his people.

## Questions for reflection

1. What things are you distracted by today that are keeping you from Jesus? What attributes of Jesus in this text could pull your focus back upon him?

2. What does it mean to you to know that you are in the same people of God as Moses?

3. Why do you think modern people downplay the importance of the local church? Why do you think church membership is so important in the life of the believer?

## PART TWO

Americans are not getting enough rest. A recent article in *Forbes* magazine argues that nearly 40% of Americans sleep less than six hours a night, leading to a higher risk for a number of health problems. Even back in 2014, the Centers for Disease Control and Prevention regarded America's sleep problem to be a public health epidemic.

But it is not just lack of physical rest that's a problem. We also need spiritual rest. The Christian life, as wonderful as it is, can also be very tiring. As we labor through the "desert" of this life, trials and tribulations can be exhausting. As humans, we are always longing for a place where we can finally rest from our spiritual journey.

Of course, God himself knows this. That's why, even in Old Testament times, he talked a lot about rest. In fact, God made a wonderful promise to the Israelites: that he would take them into the promised land of Canaan, a place of great rest. But, as we shall see below, the physical land of Canaan was not the ultimate rest God had in mind. Canaan was a picture of the great rest all believers would enjoy someday in heaven with God himself.

### A Warning Against Unbelief

Despite God's desire to give his people rest, not all received it. Our passage begins in Hebrews **3:7-11** with a warning from Psalm 95:7-11: "Today, if you hear his voice, do not harden your hearts as in the rebellion ... where your fathers put me to the test and saw my works for forty years. Therefore I was provoked with that generation, and said, 'They always go astray in their heart.'"

In this passage from Psalm 95, God is warning the reader not to make the same mistake as that wilderness generation which failed to enter the promised land—a story that would have been well known to all Jews. The Israelites had been graciously delivered out of the land of Egypt and were heading toward Canaan, a land described as flowing with milk and honey. But most never got there. They never made it to God's rest in Canaan because they were hard-hearted, rebellious, and filled with unbelief.

The grumbling came to a head in Numbers 14. Spies had been sent into Canaan and had come back with scary descriptions of its powerful inhabitants. The people were on the very edge of the promised land, but they were too afraid to enter it. They wished they had died in the desert (v 2). As a result of their disobedience, God said:

"What you have said in my hearing I will do to you: your dead bodies shall fall in this wilderness, and of all your number, listed in the census from twenty years old and upwards, who have grumbled against me, not one shall come into the land where I swore that I would make you dwell." (Numbers 14:28-30)

Hebrews **3:16-19** summarizes this well-known story by rehearsing all the reasons why the Israelites failed to enter the promised land: they "heard and yet rebelled" (**v 16**); they "sinned" (**v 17**); they "were disobedient" (**v 18**); and they exhibited "unbelief" (**v 19**).

With this story of Israel's rebellion as the backdrop, **verse 12** issues a clear warning to readers: "Take care, brothers, lest there be in any of you an evil, unbelieving heart, leading you to fall away from the living God."

Here we come to the second major warning passage in the book of Hebrews about falling away (the first being 2:1-4). Again, we should remember that to "fall away" is not a reference to a genuine believer losing their salvation. Rather it is a reference to someone inside the covenant community who seems like a believer, but later proves to have an unbelieving heart.

There are three things we should observe about this warning. First, the warning proves that *having great spiritual privileges does not guarantee true, saving faith.* If there was any group on the planet that should have believed in God, it was the Israelites. Think of all that they had seen: ten miraculous plagues, the parting of the Red Sea, manna from the sky, water from a rock, and the divine presence of God in the tabernacle. And yet, even with all those privileges, most still did not believe.

When it comes to who is saved, God has a habit of overturning our expectations. There are some who have every reason to believe and yet they don't (for example, Judas, one of Jesus' own disciples). And there are some who we think will never believe and yet they do (for example, Paul, a hater of Christians). This reminds us that salvation is in the Lord's hands: "I will have mercy on whom I have mercy" (Romans 9:15).

> We need to take the warnings seriously—while it is still "today"!

Second, *this warning applies to everyone*. Our temptation is to think to ourselves, "I don't need to listen to this warning because I believe in God." But, the Israelites could have said the same thing! For this reason, Hebrews **3:13** provides one of the cures to drifting away: "But exhort one another every day, as long as it is called 'today,' that none of you may be hardened by the deceitfulness of sin."

In other words, we need to take the warnings seriously and urgently—while it is still "today"! We should be regularly exhorting one another to press on and not drift away. Accountability is a great ally in the war against **apostasy**. We all need it.

Third, this warning teaches us that *a good start does not guarantee a good finish*. Someone might start their Christian life with excitement and optimism, but the real test is whether a person demonstrates perseverance. Thus, **verse 14** says, "For we have come to share in Christ, *if indeed we hold our original confidence firm to the end.*"

The theme of perseverance will come up again later in this passage, and throughout the book of Hebrews. Steadfastness is the test of the true believer. Jesus also made this point in his parable of the sower, when he indicated that some seed "immediately sprang up" but it didn't last because "it had no depth of soil" (Mark 4:5).

## The Promise Still Stands

With the sobering lesson of the wilderness generation still echoing in the background, our author then makes a remarkable statement in **4:1**: "The promise of entering his rest still stands." In other words, whatever rest God offered the Israelites is still available to the readers of the letter to the Hebrews (and therefore also available to us today).

Such an offer reminds us of something critical: *the ultimate rest God had in mind was not a physical plot of land.* After all, our author is not asking the readers of his letter to pack their bags and move to Canaan in order to enjoy this rest!

No, this rest that God has in mind is entered only *by faith*: "For we who have believed enter that rest" (**v 3**). Indeed, this was precisely the problem of the wilderness generation: "The message they heard did not benefit them, because they were not united by faith with those who listened" (**v 2**).

Here we learn a tremendous lesson about the way the old covenant operated: a lesson that will come up again and again later in the book of Hebrews. Although it was filled with external structures—temple, land, a physical nation—those structures pointed forward to a fuller reality found in Christit. '

The land of Canaan was not God's highest goal for his people, even in Old Testament times. His highest goal is that they would, by faith, join him in his heavenly, eternal rest.

The fact that this rest is not referring to a plot of land is confirmed later in the chapter when we are told that Joshua did *not* lead God's people into rest! **Verse 8**: "For if Joshua had given them rest, God would not have spoken of another day later on."

The point here is profound, especially for a Jewish audience that revered Joshua. Even though Joshua was famous for leading God's people into the physical land of Canaan, even crossing the Jordan miraculously (Joshua 3:1-17), he did not lead them to the *ultimate* rest God had in mind. The ultimate rest could only be achieved by another Joshua (Jesus is the Greek version of the name Joshua!) who would come at a later time to deliver his people.

In essence, then, the message of this passage is: which "Joshua" will you follow? The one who only led people to a temporary, physical rest? Or the one who will take you into eternal rest with God in heaven?

## God's Sabbath Rest

If our ultimate rest is spiritual, then what precisely does it look like? At this point, our author introduces a new way of thinking about this rest: *it is like joining God in his heavenly Sabbath*. In Hebrews **4:3-4**, we are reminded of the creation account: "His works were finished from the foundation of the world. For he has somewhere spoken of the seventh day in this way: 'And God rested on the seventh day from all his works.'"

Ever since the creation week ended, God has enjoyed a perpetual, eternal Sabbath in heaven. This doesn't mean God is inactive—he is busy in all sorts of ways (John 5:17)—but he is still resting from his work of creation. And those who believe in Jesus get to join God in this eternal Sabbath rest. Thus, we are reminded that "there remains a Sabbath rest for the people of God" (Hebrews **4:9**).

And what's so great about this eternal Sabbath? Our labors will finally come to an end: "For whoever has entered God's rest has also rested from his works as God did from his" (**v 10**). The "works" in view here are the trials and tribulations of our own journey in the "desert" on the way to the heavenly promised land. When we get to heaven, our journey is over and we can finally rest.

Of course, it should be acknowledged that we don't have to wait till heaven in order to have rest in the Christian life. As soon as we believe in Christ and the Spirit comes to dwell within us, we can enjoy a dimension of rest even in the present.

And yet, the overall thrust of the entire passage is *forward looking*. Our ultimate rest is still to come. The book of Hebrews describes this destination elsewhere in the book as "a city that has foundations, whose designer and builder is God" (11:10); "a better country, that is, a heavenly one" (11:16); and "the city of the living God, the heavenly Jerusalem" (12:22).

So, there is an "already but not yet" sense to the rest in view here. We already rest in Christ in the present, and yet we still long for, and strive for, the ultimate rest that awaits us in heaven—our real promised land.

## How Do We Enter God's Rest?

Since this promise of rest still stands, the author invites us to enter it. This requires three things from us.

The first thing we need is *faith*. As we already observed above (**4:2-3**), this was precisely the problem with the wilderness generation: they didn't believe. Israel's lack of faith is a sober reminder that we must do more than merely the hear the word. Growing up in a Christian family, doing your daily devotional, going to church—these are all good things. But they are not enough to be saved.

That said, it is important that we rightly understand the role that faith plays. It is easy to think that faith is a meritorious act, something you build up strength to do and feel proud of yourself for doing. But in fact, faith is just grabbing hold of the thing that saves us—namely, Jesus. What matters is not just faith itself but the object of our faith. What saves us is Jesus; faith is the way we get Jesus.

The second thing we need is *fear*. In other words, we need to take seriously the danger of neglecting this great offer of salvation. We see this back in the very first verse of chapter 4: "Let us fear lest any of you should seem to have failed to reach it" (**v 1**). If we want to enter into the promised land, we need to tremble; we need to have a healthy fear of ending up like the wilderness generation.

In fact, this theme pops up throughout our passage. Notice that God's rejection of that generation—"They shall not enter my rest"—is repeated in **verses 3** and **5**. Also, we are reminded again in **verse 6** that the Israelites "failed to enter because of disobedience." And then in **verse 7** the author quotes the sober warning of Psalm 95 yet again: "Today, if you hear his voice, do not harden your hearts."

The point is hard to miss. Be sober and serious about making sure you don't end up like the Israelites, dying in the desert and failing to enter God's rest.

Our modern world needs this message more than ever. Few today take spiritual matters seriously. Thoughts of eternity are dismissed with a wave of the hand, as if such things will just work themselves out in the end. Sadly, such an approach is precisely what the author is warning us against.

Instead, we should remember that "today" is the day of salvation. Do not put off examining your heart and reflecting upon your eternal status. How does one do that? Well, the passage suggests one way: Israel's lack of faith was evident in their disobedience (Hebrews **4:6**). While we are not saved by our obedience—we are only saved by faith in Christ—our obedience can be a test of whether our faith is real. Indeed, when Jesus explained how to spot false teachers, he said, "You will recognize them by their fruits" (Matthew 7:16).

So, how's the fruit of obedience in your life today? No Christian can be perfect this side of glory; we all fall far short of God's perfect standard. But if someone truly believes in Christ and is filled with his Spirit, they will inevitably produce good fruit (Matthew 13:23).

The third thing we need is *fight*. Why? Because the Christian life can be hard. Yes, it can be wonderful, exciting, and fulfilling. But it can also be exhausting, disheartening, and discouraging. If we are going to make it through the desert and to the promised land, it will take effort.

In fact, this is how this section of chapter 4 ends: "Let us therefore strive to enter that rest" (Hebrews **4:11**). The word "strive" is important here. It reminds us that effort, diligence, and perseverance are essential to the Christian life. No, we are not saved by our efforts—we are only saved by the grace of Christ. But the Christian life still involves effort! It is not passive and detached but active and intentional.

This is why the book of Hebrews will later compare the Christian life to running a race (12:1). Running does not come easy. It takes hard work and sacrifice to push through the pain and the exhaustion.

But there is a great reward at the end. There is a great promised land waiting for you. One day, there will be no more striving, no more temptations, no more trials. There will be peace and rest forever with Jesus. "Whoever has entered God's rest has also rested from his works as God did from his" (**4:10**). This is our great hope today.

## Questions **for reflection**

1. What causes you to doubt, grumble, or complain in your relationship with God?

2. Do you find yourself with an appropriate level of fear when you think about your eternal future? What are some ways in which we can wake up from our complacency?

3. How does this passage help you see that effort and striving are good and necessary parts of the Christian life? What are some ways in which you can "fight" for your faith today?

# 4. THE LIVING WORD AND THE PERFECT PRIEST

On October 31, 1517, a German monk named Martin Luther nailed his 95 **theses** to the door of the Wittenberg Church. That singular event was the tiny spark that lit an enormous fire that spread throughout all of Europe, and even all of the world. It began what we now call the Protestant Reformation.

Years later, Luther wrote about what made it all happen. What was it exactly that led to this great transformation of the world? Luther's answer captures the essence of the Reformation:

"I simply taught, preached and wrote God's Word. Otherwise I did nothing … The Word so greatly weakened the **papacy** that no prince or emperor ever inflicted such losses upon it. I did nothing; the Word did everything."

(*Luther's Works*, Volume 51, p 77)

The world wasn't changed through political maneuvering or a big army or lots of money but by the power of the word of God. That is God's main instrument to change the world—and to change us personally.

Hebrews **4:12-13** captures this truth in one of the most profound passages in the Bible. It is one of the best summaries of what makes God's word so special.

At first glance, it may seem that these verses are out of place, as though our author suddenly changes topic. But they flow quite directly from the prior verses. Recall that in verse 11, we received yet another warning that we should obey God, lest we fall away like the Israelites. And then in **verses 12** and **13** the author explains why we should listen to God: because his word is living, active, and powerful. It is always trustworthy and true.

## The Danger of Disbelief

Before diving further into this passage, we should pause to observe that this theme—God speaking his word to his people—has marked the book of Hebrews from the very beginning. Remember how the letter began: "Long ago … *God spoke.*" Then, in chapter 3, the author gave a particular instance of God speaking to his people as he cited Psalm 95:7-11. That passage recounts how God spoke to his people in the desert and they didn't listen to him.

Thus, when our author uses the phrase "the word of God" in Hebrews **4:12**, he is no doubt referring back to the promises made in Psalm 95. God was inviting his people to join him in his rest, but they didn't listen. They did not believe God, and as a result they did not enter his rest (3:19). This promise of rest is open to us too, and the way of entering it is the same: believing God's word.

Whether or not to believe God's word is not merely a technical, academic question. No, it is a question of salvation. It is a question of eternity. 4:11 tells us that if we do not trust God and believe the promises he offers in the gospel, then what happened to the Israelites will happen to us: we may "fall."

Have you ever thought about how remarkable it is that the Israelites did not believe, even after all they had experienced? Even those who had witnessed the pillar of fire that led them through the desert, and the sea parting, and water springing from a rock, would not believe. We, who have not seen these things, need to realize that unbelief is a danger in our lives too. It is a problem with every human heart.

We doubt God's promises for many reasons. Perhaps we think our way is better—we decide that with our small, fallible minds, we understand the universe better than God does. Perhaps it is the fact that God does not always bring about his promises instantaneously; he moves at his own pace, and we become impatient. Perhaps it is listening to false teachers—people who distort God's word and confuse us about it. Perhaps it is the messages we hear from the world, telling us that God's word is not really trustworthy and that a rich, full existence can be found elsewhere. Perhaps it is experiencing a terrible trial, which leads us to think, "If God let this happen to me, he can't be real."

Whatever the trigger, we all have a propensity in our fallen hearts to doubt God's promises. So, the author of Hebrews needs to reassure us that God's word is worthy of our trust. He accomplishes this by laying out three attributes of God's word. It is personal, it is powerful, and it is penetrating.

## God's Word Is Personal

Sometimes we have a tendency to view the Bible as just a book filled with helpful information. It is like a religious encyclopedia: if you want to get facts about Jesus, about God, or about salvation, then this is the reference tool you use. As a result, the Bible can seem a bit stale, static, or even lifeless.

But **verse 12** begins with a remarkable declaration which shatters this misunderstanding: the word of God is *living*. What does that mean? It means that a living person is revealed in it. Since God's word is empowered by the Holy Spirit, when we encounter the word, we encounter God. It is through God's word that we meet him, learn from him, and have fellowship with him.

In this way, the word is remarkably *personal*.

Theologian John Frame captures this wonderfully:

"When we encounter the word of God, we encounter God ... His word, indeed, is his personal presence. Whenever God's word is spoken, read, or heard, God himself is there."

(*The Doctrine of the Word of God*, p 88)

It is not that the paper and the binding are somehow divine. The Bibles we hold in our hands are just physical objects. But when the content of the message and the words themselves take root in our hearts, God is meeting his people.

This highlights what makes the Bible different from every other book. Imagine, for example, that you went to the library and checked out a book about Abraham Lincoln. In that book, you may learn a lot of facts about him—his upbringing, political career, role in the Civil War, and so on. But there is one thing you will never get in a book about Lincoln: *you will never meet him.*

That is not the case with the word of God, whose author is not dead. By the power of the Spirit, God manifests himself in the words of Scripture. This is the stunning difference between the Bible and every other book in the world. God's presence is actually encountered in his word. This is a personal, living book.

This reality has implications for why we think the Bible is true. We typically believe that the Bible is true for very impersonal reasons: it conforms to the facts of history, has reliable manuscripts, and so on. But we can also believe that the Bible is true for personal reasons: because we recognize that it contains the voice of someone we know and trust. Jesus said as much: "My sheep hear my voice, and I know them, and they follow me" (John 10:27).

> The word of God is energetic, powerful, and mighty. It doesn't just say things; it *does* things.

A second implication is that there is no place for statements such as "I like Jesus, but not the Bible." In the Western world today, we are seeing the rise of popular spirituality, which is a way to feel that you are contacting God while bypassing the means which God has given for that. People say that they do not want to be constrained by the Bible; they do not believe in the authority of God's word but only in their own personal experience. But God has manifested himself in his word. That is the primary way of meeting and interacting with him.

A third implication is that we need to recognize that any encounter with the Bible is a serious matter. If God's power is manifest through his word, then studying the Bible is not to be taken lightly. We don't want to tinker around with the Bible as if it's a hobby. When we encounter the word, we are encountering the Lord of the universe—and that is a sobering thing to consider. This ought to shift the way we think about how we study his word.

## God's Word Is Powerful

The second feature of God's word is that it is powerful. It is not just living but also "active." The word "active" in Greek is *energes*, which is where our English word "energy" comes from. The word of God is energetic, powerful, and mighty. It doesn't just say things; it *does* things. It is busy working, changing, building, convicting, encouraging, exposing, rebuking, giving light and wisdom, carving out the path of our lives, and showing us the truth of God.

At the very beginning, God spoke the world into existence. When Jesus was tempted in the wilderness, he used the power and energy of God's word to rebuke and push back the lies of the devil. Then there are Jesus' miracles, performed by speaking. "**Lazarus**, come out" was a divine decree (John 11:43). Jesus calmed the sea simply by saying to the waves, "Be still" (Mark 4:39).

This is the kind of thing that the word still does. We don't have Jesus standing beside us physically anymore, but we do have his words in the Scriptures, and those words are "active." 2 Timothy 3:16-17 tells us, "All Scripture is breathed out by God and profitable for teaching, for reproof, for correction, and for training in righteousness, that the **man of God** may be complete, equipped for every good work." Scripture is sufficient for all this—it is everything you need in order to live a life of godliness and service of Christ (2 Peter 1:3). It is so powerful, so energetic, and does so many things that it can help you with any problem in your life. It equips you for every good work.

Yet we turn to other things. Have you noticed how big the self-help section is in most bookstores today? Have you seen the amount of "life advice" content there is on social media? While such things can sometimes provide helpful **common-grace** insights, people are missing out on the all-sufficient power of God's word. We should not doubt that God's word is powerful enough to accomplish in our lives whatever is needed.

## God's Word Is Penetrating

This leads us to the third feature of God's word: it is penetrating. It is "sharper than any two-edged sword." This is the crescendo; all the rest of Hebrews **4:12-13** relates to this.

The reference to a "two-edged sword" would have been one that the audience recognized. No doubt the author was referring to the Roman short sword—known as a *gladius*. This was not the long sword that we typically think of from the times of knights and castles. No, this was the standard sword for the Roman legions, short but sharp, and designed to cut through the enemy's armor in close combat.

Likewise, God's word is designed to cut. Indeed, it is made to penetrate the hardest substance on the planet—not granite or diamonds but something even harder: the human heart.

We know this, of course, because we've likely tried to reach another person's heart and found it to be hardened by sin and impossible to touch. We've even tried to reach our own heart and realized that it, too, can be stubborn and intractable. As a result, sometimes we just give up and try to change the outside rather than the inside. So we put on a show, play a part, look like a good Christian, go to church; but on the inside, things may remain a mess.

We know that true change, lasting change, has to start with the heart. And the only thing sharp enough to touch it is God's word, empowered by the Spirit. It pierces "to the division of soul and of spirit, of joints and of marrow" (**v 12**). It is like a surgeon's knife: incredibly precise and razor-sharp. Unlike any literal sword, it is able to cut the soul. If you want to reach people in your life—if you want to reach yourself—this is the thing to do it with. God has given you this divine instrument which has been designed to affect the heart.

So, if the purpose of God's word is to penetrate the heart, what does it do once it gets there? It exposes who we really are: "discerning the thoughts and intentions of the heart." The word of God is not just a way to get to know God but also a way to get to know yourself. When you read the Bible and let it penetrate your heart, you will see things about yourself that you never saw before. You will see your real intentions, your real motives, and your real character. This is a good thing because there is rot and mildew built up in our hearts which need to be exposed.

We all make resolutions about how we would like to change, but we cannot change ourselves unless we have an accurate perception of where we are starting from. The word of God gives us that. It lays it all bare. We try to hide who we really are from each other, from ourselves, and from God. But **verse 13** tells us that "no creature is hidden from his sight." The word of God will show you who you really are and what your real problems are. It will get into your heart and heal it.

Why does that matter? Because if you don't deal with those things in your heart that are tripping you up, then you might find yourself like the Israelites—doubting, disbelieving and turning away from the living God. God's word does surgery on your soul in order to prevent you from falling away and losing the rest that God has promised you.

In his word God is personally present; through his word he powerfully acts; and by his word he penetrates to the place that no human can ever reach—the human heart. All that together makes one simple point. Is God's word trustworthy? Should we rely on it and believe its promises? The answer is absolutely "Yes."

## Questions for reflection

1. In what ways are you being tempted to doubt the truth of God's word today? Or in what ways have you questioned its power?

2. How should we study the Bible differently, or listen to preaching differently, given that it manifests the living presence of God himself?

3. What are some steps you can take in the coming months to make sure you are learning, receiving, and listening to the word of God?

## PART TWO

### A High Priest Like No Other

In Hebrews **4:14** our author comes back to the theme of Christ as high priest, which we last saw in 3:1. He is showing us that Jesus is better than the Old Testament high priests. This time we are given more details about why that is the case, and about the difference it makes to us.

All of us are in a perilous position as we stand before the holy court of God. We need somebody to speak for us, act for us, intercede for us, and represent us. In the West, where everybody values independence, self-reliance, and the do-it-yourself mentality, we easily end up applying that to religion too. But the message of Hebrews **4:14 – 5:10** is that we need an intercessor.

The ancient Israelites had earthly high priests, who went before God on behalf of the people, and so they already had a sense that they needed such a person—that they couldn't stand before the holy God on their own merits. But what we will find out is that those earthly high priests didn't really get the job done. They only pointed toward the real, ultimate high priest—Jesus.

In **4:14-16** we will see three things that we need in a high priest in order to enable us to go before the throne of God confidently. Then **5:1-10** expands on this with a direct comparison between Jesus and all other high priests. Christ not only fulfills all qualifications for a high priest but actually surpasses them. And he is a model for our own lives as we seek to serve God and minister to others.

### Effective Intercession

In ancient Israel, the earthly high priest would go into a little room in the middle of the temple called the Most Holy Place. There is a sense in which God's presence was in that place; but at the same time, it was just a man-made building. It was a symbol of how man needs an intercessor between himself and God—someone to represent one to the other.

The high priest would enter once a year on the **Day of Atonement** and make a sacrifice for the people of God (see Leviticus 16). But this is not what Jesus did. The reason why he is a better high priest is because he presented himself as an **intercessor** in God's own personal presence in the heavenly places. He "passed through the heavens" (Hebrews **4:14**), entering not a man-made building but the real heavenly temple itself. (The author will pick up this point later, starting in 9:24.)

In other words, Christ has unique *access* to God—and therefore he can be with him in order to plead our case. He alone has the standing with God to be the intercessor we need. His intercession is effective.

But there is a second reason that Jesus' intercession is so effective. The difference is made not just by *where* he does it but also by *how long* he does it for. Notice the language the author uses: he says, "Jesus, the Son of God." He adds that title here very particularly. Jesus can intercede for us forever because he is the eternal Son of God.

If you are a follower of Jesus, he will never, ever stop loving you, pleading your case, and representing you before God. That means that when God looks at us, he sees the righteousness of his Son surrounding us. That is what it means to be represented by Jesus, and that never stops. We can have eternal security in heaven because we have someone who is able to intercede for us forever.

The implication of that comes at the end of **4:14**: "Let us hold fast our confession." Do not abandon what you believe about Jesus, because there is nothing better to turn to than this intercessor.

## Full Sympathy

Jesus is the Son of God: eternal, divine, glorious. But can he relate to me? What we need is a high priest who not only enters heaven but also comes to earth. We need someone who has experienced what we experience and can sympathize with us. And this is what is amazing about Jesus. He doesn't just act God-ward; he acts man-ward.

The author has already mentioned this point in 2:17-18, but here he breaks it down.

First, he sympathizes with our "weaknesses" (**4:15**). Jesus did not shield himself from the fallenness of the world. He was "despised and rejected by men, a man of sorrows and acquainted with grief" (Isaiah 53:3). He really did experience everything in this life that is dark and difficult and prob-

> We need to realize that we have an eternal well of sympathy and compassion in Christ.

lematic, from physical suffering to relational troubles. And when he hung on the cross, he was not only scorned by all around him but drank from the cup of his Father's wrath—wrath that was poured out on him in the place of sinners.

Second, "in every respect [he] has been tempted as we are." He was tempted by Satan in the wilderness: tempted by wealth, by power, and by comfort. He was tempted in the garden of Gethsemane to avoid suffering. Whatever you are tempted by, Jesus can relate to you in this way as well.

This means that Christ is the one we should come to for sympathy and compassion.

We spend a lot of our time and energy trying to solicit compassion from others, putting on display reasons why we deserve more sympathy and attention than other people. We have a deep human desire for sympathy. What we need to realize is that we have an eternal well of sympathy and compassion in Christ.

Once we realize this, we are freed to show deep compassion and sympathy to others. If we have drunk deeply of the compassion available to us in Christ, we no longer have to find ways to get it from others. Go to Christ, who fully sympathizes with your weaknesses, and then you can serve others by showing them the very sympathy and compassion that was shown to you.

## True Purification

The last phrase of Hebrews **4:15** is very important. Jesus was "without sin." Unlike any other high priest—unlike any other human—Christ has no sins of his own. He is the perfect man.

Jesus' perfection and purity are important because his righteous deeds are credited to our account. By your faith in Jesus, God looks at you and views you as a pure person. You are perfect in his eyes because Christ's righteousness covers you and wraps around you. All of this hangs on the fact that Christ was sinless.

The result is that we can "with confidence draw near to the throne of grace" (**v 16**). This is not the confidence that says, "I'll be fine before God because I'm a pretty good person." No, this is confidence not in yourself but in Christ and in his perfect representation. You can march right into the throne room of God, saying, "I am God's child. Jesus has saved me." We have amazing access to God by virtue of what Christ has done.

## Beset with Weakness

In chapter 5 the writer to the Hebrews develops the theme of Christ's priesthood more fully—why he is able to fully purify us from sin.

The author reminds us that Old Testament priests were human: "chosen from among men" (**5:1**). It was important that they experienced life like everyone else: the fallenness of the world, the problems, the temptations, the weaknesses and so on. This enabled them to "deal gently with the ignorant and wayward" (**v 2**).

But the disadvantage of the priests' weakness was that it meant they sinned too. Therefore, when they made offerings, they did not just make them on behalf of the people. They had to make offerings on their own behalf (**v 3**).

We have already seen what the big difference is when it comes to Jesus. He is able to sympathize with our weaknesses, "yet without sin" (4:15). So he can relate, but unlike the priests he can also save. For this reason, he surpasses the Old Testament priests.

**5:7-9** are tremendous verses which illustrate this similarity and difference.

The language in **verse 7**—"prayers and **supplications**, with loud cries and tears"—likely refers to Jesus' cries to his Father in the Garden of Gethsemane (Luke 22:41-44). So much did he dread what was coming—the wrath of his own Father—that his sweat was like drops of blood. This is the stress and the sorrow that Jesus endured. His suffering was very, very real.

But Jesus was without sin. He "was heard because of his reverence." The Greek word translated "reverence" here captures a posture of submission before the Father. Submission is not easy; it is needed when you don't want to do something or you don't want to do it a particular way. It means willingly, humbly recognizing the authority of another over you.

Jesus' cries expressed his willingness to submit to whatever God had prepared for him—however difficult it would be. His obedience was radical. God heard his prayer: "Remove this cup from me" (Luke 22:42). But he did not release him from suffering. God said no. And Jesus submitted to that, too.

The word "submission" is not a popular word today, but the Bible praises submission in all kinds of areas. God calls us to submit to whatever authorities are in our life (Titus 3:1): to our pastors and **elders** (Hebrews 13:17), to our government (1 Peter 2:13-14; Romans 13:1-6), and most importantly to our Father in heaven (James 4:7).

When God tells you no, it is hard to submit. But Christ models for us submission to what might be the greatest "no" that anybody has ever received.

The school of suffering is not an easy one. But it can teach us, train us, and shape us like no other school, making us more effective ministers to others. It can help to make us more sympathetic and compassionate. We are told that even Jesus "learned obedience through what he suffered" (Hebrews **5:8**).

Of course, this language raises a natural question. How is it that Jesus "learned" obedience? Wasn't he always perfect? Yes, he was always perfect. But to say Jesus learned obedience is not to suggest he was at one time disobedient. Rather it emphasizes Jesus' experience as a human being who learned what it was like to obey God even in the midst of great suffering—an experience that allowed him, at a later point, to be "obedient to the point of death, even death on a cross" (Philippians 2:8).

Jesus' example is the one to follow when we are suffering. We can, like him, ask the Father to relieve us and comfort us. But whether the answer is yes or no, we must remain obedient to God. And—praise God—we can remember that we have a great high priest who is able to sympathize with our weaknesses. We can with confidence draw near to him in prayer, asking for mercy and grace to help us in our need (Hebrews **4:16**).

## The Source of Salvation

Jesus' suffering and obedience meant that he was "made perfect" (**5:9**). This doesn't mean that Christ was made perfect morally or ethically: he was always sinless. He was made perfect in the sense that he was made our perfect high priest. His suffering and obedience made him a better representative for us. And as a result, "he became the source of eternal salvation to all who obey him."

This is how Jesus truly purifies us. His obedience is the reason why we have hope in his representation. He did not fall or waver or give up: he was obedient. He remained sinless, and that meant that he could be a sacrifice on our behalf instead of having to pay for his own sins. And his righteousness, his obedience, and his faithfulness are credited to us when we trust in him.

Whenever you read the Gospels, when you see Jesus' obedience and purity, remember that he was winning salvation for us. Every time he obeyed, that was part of the redemption he has achieved for us. The crux comes poignantly at Gethsemane, where no doubt Satan wanted him to abandon his obedience. But Jesus stayed the course through suffering, becoming the perfect high priest that we desperately need.

## Called by God

**Verses 4-6** reveal another way in which Jesus was like the Old Testament high priest but better.

Priests were not self-appointed—they had to be called by God (**v 4**). We might think that that would not apply to Jesus. He is the Son of God, so he should not need to be humble and wait to be appointed by God. But the amazing thing is that Jesus was humble. He, too, was called. This is what we see laid out in the following verses. "Christ did not exalt himself to be made a high priest, but was appointed" (**v 5**).

To prove that Jesus was called, the author once again turns to the Old Testament, quoting both Psalm 2 and Psalm 110 (in Hebrews **5:5** and **5:6** respectively). Psalm 2 is a well-known messianic psalm that pictures the coming Messiah as both a priest and a king—a theme that will surface again later. Psalm 110 features Melchizedek, who is an important forerunner of Jesus because he was also a priest-king. We will return to this figure soon, in Hebrews 6:20 and into chapter 7.

But, for now, the main point to glean from these verses is that Jesus was appointed by God to this task. As glorious as he was, he did not appoint himself. He submitted to the Father not only in Gethsemane but also when he first came to earth—and in everything he did (John 6:38).

This principle of humility applies to us too. It is all too common to find self-appointed people in ministry who seek honor for themselves:

they put on a show, surround themselves with people who love them, and take no advice from anyone else. This attitude is a danger for all of us, not just those who are in ministry. How much do we worry about how we look and what people think about us, rather than how Christ looks and what people think about him? Our job is to glorify Christ, not win the praise of man. Our number one goal should be to please God—as Jesus' was.

Christ submitted obediently to the trials of suffering; he humbled himself to glorify his Father. He fulfills—and surpasses—the qualifications of a high priest in ancient Israel. What a great high priest we have, and what a great model for our own service.

## Questions for reflection

1. In what ways have you tried to represent yourself before God, rather than letting Jesus do that?

2. What keeps you from being sure of your standing with God? How does this passage help?

3. How are you encouraged today by the fact that Jesus took on human flesh and suffered like us?

# 5. A SOBER WARNING

Whatever happened to Susan Pevensie? If you are a fan of C.S. Lewis's *Chronicles of Narnia*, you will know that Susan is one of the main characters in *The Lion, the Witch, and the Wardrobe*—one of the four children who end up as kings and queens of Narnia. But in the very last book of the series, *The Last Battle*, in a scene which effectively represents heaven, you realize that Susan is not there. It is a glaring, jarring omission. Even within the story, other characters ask why Susan is not there in glory with the rest.

Here is the answer:

"'My sister Susan,' answered Peter shortly and gravely, 'is no longer a friend of Narnia.'

'Yes,' said Eustace, 'and whenever you try to get her to come and talk about Narnia or do anything about Narnia, she says, "What wonderful memories you have! Fancy you still thinking about all those funny games we used to play when we were children."'" (p 154)

This scene raises a very important issue. When we get to heaven, there will be people whom we expected to see there but we won't see them—people we thought were believers who turn out not to be. Lewis is describing someone who seemed to be a follower of Aslan—who seemed, in other words, to be a Christian—but who ends up turning away. Eustace's words explain why: she dismisses all their childhood memories as mere games, as if they didn't really happen.

Susan is trying to be a grown-up now and no longer a child. She is on to other things.

In the Christian life, this is called apostasy. An apostate is someone who once seemed to be a believer, but who later totally rejects Christ, turns away from sound teaching, and leaves the church. Apostasy is a real, sobering, scary, weighty issue. And it is the one that God puts right before us in Hebrews 5:11 – 6:12.

The writer starts off by saying, *I'm worried about you* (**5:11-14**). His audience is not maturing as quickly as expected. And he is concerned about their spiritual health. In **6:1-3**, he encourages them to move on and grow up in their faith. Then in **6:4-8** he dives into the very difficult theme of apostasy. He explains that those who seemed to be believers, yet have fallen away, will be subject to God's severe judgment.

> If you are not growing in your Christian life, then that should be a wake-up call.

It is important to clarify again that true believers cannot lose their salvation. If someone is truly saved, truly regenerate, and truly trusting in Christ, they will always be held fast by him (John 10:28). However, God uses warnings of apostasy to encourage his people to stay the course of faith. So as we read this passage, we should carefully ponder it, absorb it, and learn from it as we reflect upon our own spiritual maturity. This is what the writer to the Hebrews helps his readers to do later on, in Hebrews **6:9-12**. He cites the good signs of spiritual growth that he sees in them and encourages them to persevere in the faith.

This passage may seem like a detour, but really it is not. As we know, the whole theme of the book of Hebrews is to say that Christ is better: superior to the old covenant revelation and superior to anything else you might worship, love, or adore. So, the whole book functions as a warning against apostasy. It is about calling people to

Christ and saying, *Don't drift away. Don't give up. Don't go chasing other things.*

## Spiritual Immaturity

Imagine a grown adult who only drinks milk and has never moved on to solid food. If you met such a person you would think that something must be seriously wrong.

But that is exactly what our author says his readers are like, spiritually speaking. They should really be eating solid food by now, but they are still drinking bottles of milk (**5:12**). In other words, they are languishing in immaturity. They are not advancing down the path of growth which a Christian ought to advance down. It's as if they are still toddlers.

If you are not growing in your Christian life, then that should be a wake-up call. If your growth has stalled, then you are putting yourself in a vulnerable position spiritually.

The writer gives four characteristics of these spiritual toddlers. They don't listen very well; they are forgetful; they are unskilled; and they are undiscerning. That is actually a pretty good description of any toddler! They don't listen to you, they forget what you tell them, they can't do anything for themselves, and they have no idea of what is right or wrong, safe or dangerous. That is the spiritual condition of the original readers of this letter.

## 1. They Don't Listen

In the preceding verses, the author has just begun to talk about Jesus as a high priest in the order of Melchizedek. But he interrupts himself in **verse 11**: "About this we have much to say, and it is hard to explain." Why does he say that these things are hard to explain? It is not that his readers are not very smart. It is not because these theological concepts are so intricate and complex that they go way over people's heads. No, it is because the Christians he is writing to are "dull of hearing."

The word "dull" really just means "lazy." It's not that they are unable to listen; they are not bothering to listen. "Numb" would also be a good translation. Have you ever found yourself hearing the word of God in a sermon but feeling numb, zoned out, a little bit lazy? That is what the writer is talking about.

We all know that there are good preachers and bad preachers. But when we think about our approach to listening to sermons, many of us need to spend less time critiquing the style of the preacher and more time asking ourselves, "Am I a good listener?" We should say to ourselves: "Even if the talk was difficult to follow or badly delivered, was I listening to what God said there? Was I listening to his word?"

Our author's readers are not listening. They are lazy, numb, and checked out when they hear the word—the **theology** that the writer is giving them. They are not interested in understanding God's plan of salvation and how Jesus is the greatest high priest. And it is a sign of spiritual unhealth in a person when they hear theology and good **doctrine** and say, "Who cares?"

## 2. They Are Forgetful

The readers of this letter, it seems, did not remember what they had been told. They were having to be taught the same things over and over and over again; so the writer says, "You need someone to teach you again the basic principles" (**v 12**). They were not growing because they were letting good teaching just drift out of their minds.

This forgetfulness is actually a sign of selfishness. The audience of this letter "ought to be teachers" by now. Instead they have become only takers in the church and not givers. They have become high-maintenance toddler Christians.

Do toddlers help with the dishes? No. Do they clean their rooms? No. Do they prepare their own food? No. All these things have to be done for them. Toddlers are almost one hundred percent takers. That's not their fault—they're toddlers! But if you are still acting like that when you're 35, something is seriously wrong.

It is the same with spiritual health and growth. Have you got to the point where you're not just taking but actually starting to give back? Are you serving others? Are you helping others to learn? Or are you like a grown-up toddler?

## 3. They Are Unskilled

Spiritual toddlers, living on spiritual milk and not solid food, are "unskilled in the word of righteousness" (**v 13**). The phrase "word of righteousness" just means God's word; so, these people have not learned how to rightly understand the word of God. They have not grown in their knowledge of the word of God. They are unskilled—like little children.

The Bible is more widely available now than it has ever been. You can get it in any format you want. Many people have multiple printed copies; and now you can also have it on your phone or tablet. The Bible has never been more accessible. Yet I don't think Western people have ever been at a point where they know it less. I am not talking about our society in general; I am talking about Christians who are simply unskilled in the word of God.

Now, this is not to suggest that a person has to be a Bible scholar in order to be a Christian. That's not what our author is saying. But if you are not growing in your knowledge of God through his word, then you are an immature believer—and that is a dangerous thing to be.

One of the most basic things you can do to grow in that particular area is to be a reader. Since you are reading this book, I presume that you are already committed to knowing God's word better. I'm excited for you! But I would encourage us all to keep asking ourselves, "Am I a student of God's word in a way that is maturing and growing me?"

We need to think of ourselves as lifelong learners. We should always be growing in the knowledge of God.

## 4. They Are Undiscerning

In **verse 14**, the author describes people who are the opposite of the immature Christians he is writing to—those who are mature and eat solid food. These are "those who have their powers of discernment trained by constant practice to distinguish good from evil."

Here's the nub of the matter. If you are an immature Christian, you cannot always separate right from wrong. If you are not a good listener, if you are selfish and forgetful, if you are not skilled in God's word, and if you are not maturing, then you are susceptible to deception. You cannot distinguish good from evil very effectively—like a toddler who runs out into the street, unaware of the danger.

This is what leads to the possibility of apostasy. If you are not growing in your Christian faith, you could be much more easily enticed away by deceptions because you don't have the strength and the energy to defend yourself.

Have you ever seen a documentary of lions hunting wildebeest in the Serengeti? You'll notice that they always go for the newborns first. The baby wildebeest who can hardly hold themselves up and are just trying to keep up with their mothers—those are the ones the lions can easily separate from the herd and bring down.

It is the same in the Christian life. If you are not growing up in your faith, you are more susceptible to those who want to trick and deceive you and take you down wrong paths.

My challenge to you is to look over those four characteristics and do a little spiritual assessment of your own Christian growth.

Ask yourself: If I look back at myself five years ago, is there any difference now? Can I see God's work in me? Am I moving closer to God and not further from him? Am I serving those around me? Am I growing in the **fruit of the Spirit** (Galatians 5:22-23)? Am I helping others to learn the truth? Am I growing in my understanding of God?

Of course, we are saved by grace alone through faith alone. We have the love of Christ because of his merits, not ours. Growth is not about earning God's affection. Yet he does want us to grow up.

In this way, God is like any parent. No father says to a little toddler, "If you don't grow up, I'm going to stop loving you." Nor does a mother say, "When you grow up, I'll love you more." No, a good parent loves that toddler with an endless love already. Of course, they want him or her to grow up and to mature. But even if the toddler never really does grow up, it will not mean he or she is any less loved.

## Strive for Growth

In Hebrews **6:1-3**, the writer adds a hopeful encouragement, telling us to strive toward spiritual growth. **Verse 1** says, "Therefore let us leave the elementary doctrine of Christ and go on to maturity."

When he says "leave the elementary doctrine," he doesn't mean leave it behind altogether. What he means is build on it; add to it. Elementary doctrines are very important. But you cannot just be satisfied with milk forever. You have to get onto the solid food.

What are these elementary doctrines? Three of them are mentioned in **verse 2**. First, "repentance and faith." This is just a reference to how you become a Christian. You repented and believed. Second, "instruction about washings, the laying on of hands." This is probably a reference to baptism and entrance to the church. (Sometimes the laying on of hands, associated with **baptism**, was a symbolic gesture indicating that one had received the Spirit.) Third, "the resurrection of the dead, and eternal judgment." This is the Christian's understanding of the fact that Christ will come again to judge the world, and that those who love him will spend eternity with him.

These are core doctrines. These are the things that every Christian, however immature, knows. But what our author is saying is that you cannot just stop there. So, he gives his audience a final push: "And this we will do if God permits" (**v 3**).

I come across so many people in the church who may be true believers, but the understanding they have of their faith is still at this simple level. They know that the gospel requires repentance and faith. They have joined the church, they have been baptized, and they are looking forward to Christ's second coming. And that is where it all stops. Of course, those are great truths. But there is so much more to learn! There is so much more growth possible. There are great meals to eat. Don't be satisfied with milk when you could be enjoying a wonderful steak dinner.

## **Questions** for reflection

1. Do you know people in your life who have apostatized? How did that impact your own spiritual life?

2. Honestly appraise your own spiritual maturity. In what ways are you still like a toddler and need to grow? In what ways do your areas of immaturity make you vulnerable to attack?

3. What are some concrete steps you can take to move beyond the ABCs of the Christian faith?

# PART TWO

Until Christ returns, there will always be some in the church who seem to be true believers but are not. Jesus warns us about this in Matthew 7:22: "On that day, many will say to me, 'Lord, Lord, did we not prophesy in your name, and cast out demons in your name, and do many mighty works in your name?' And then will I declare to them, 'I never knew you; depart from me.'" There will be people who think they are Christians but later prove not to be.

These are some of the most difficult verses in the entire book of Hebrews: the most controversial and most debated. We could spend five chapters on this one section, going through all the different options and views! But let me whittle it down as simply as I can.

## Those Who Seem Like True Believers

First, it is often said that the portrayal of the person in Hebrews **6:4-5** sounds like that of a true Christian. But of course it sounds like that! That's the whole point of the passage: namely, that there can be people who look a lot like Christians but then later prove not to be. Before someone apostatizes, they look like a true believer. As we noted above, it was not obvious to the other disciples that Judas would betray Jesus. They never saw it coming.

Each of the phrases in these verses comes very close to describing a Christian, but when we examine them, we find that they are not evidence of someone who really has a **regenerate** new heart and is saved by Christ.

We should remember that there were people like this in Old Testament Israel: many were part of God's chosen nation, but they were not part of the true Israel. They weren't really saved. Think of the exodus story, which we explored in Hebrews 3 and 4. Despite being delivered from Egypt, many Israelites never made it into the promised land but died in the desert due to their unbelief. In fact, I'm convinced that in this passage, the story of Israel in the desert is still on the author's mind.

Think of all the experiences that the average Israelite had during the time of the exodus. The parting of the Red Sea; a column of fire leading them by night and a cloud by day; water coming from a rock at Moses' command; **manna** appearing each morning. There is the moment when Moses comes down from the mountain with his face shining so brightly that the people cannot look at it. There is the thunder they can hear from the mountain. There are the Ten Commandments.

All these things are impressive evidence for God. Yet there were those who saw all that and experienced all that, and still fell away. This is what an apostate is: someone who has experienced that many blessings yet still says, "No, thank you. I don't believe it."

So, let us turn our attention now to the four blessings or privileges which our author mentions to describe someone who seems to be a believer but really isn't.

## 1. They were once "enlightened" (**6:4**).

This word "enlightened" is also used later in the book of Hebrews to refer to those who have received the knowledge of God's truth (10:32, 26). That's true of an apostate—initially. Think of the parable of the sower (Matthew 13:1-23). Some of the seeds fall on rocky ground and the plants sprout up quickly; some of the seeds fall among thorns and grow there too. But they never bear fruit; they get scorched or choked and die. What this means is that it is possible to initially receive God's truth and understand it—to be "enlightened"—but later to fall away.

## 2. They have "tasted the heavenly gift."

It's a little unclear what exactly "the heavenly gift" is. The blessings of God's covenant community, perhaps. The word "heavenly" may be an echo of the manna from heaven that the Israelites enjoyed. Or the word "tasted" may be a reference to the **Lord's Supper**. Regardless of all the options here, this is yet another example of someone who's been blessed in some way in God's community and has participated in God's church.

3. They have "shared in the Holy Spirit" (**v 4**) and tasted "the powers of the age to come" (**v 5**).

You can share in what the Spirit is doing in a congregation, even if you are not yourself saved and indwelt by the Spirit. You can see and benefit from the blessings of the Spirit as he brings spiritual gifts into those around you in the congregation; or as the Spirit displays powerful signs and wonders ("powers of the age to come").

There's also a sense in which non-Christians can exhibit certain kinds of spiritual giftedness, as mysterious as that may be. A good example of this is King Saul. He was one who was given great spiritual privileges by God—not only leading his people but also prophesying (1 Samuel 10:11)—yet he ended up rejecting God's ways. Judas is another good example. He was one of the twelve whom Jesus sent out to perform miracles and to cast out demons (Matthew 10:1-4), and we are not told that he failed to do so. Strange as it sounds, there is a sense in which a person can share in some sort of spiritual activity even as an unbeliever.

4. They have tasted the goodness of the word of God.

Week after week, apostates sit under the teaching of the word and hear the blessings of preaching. God speaks his truth to them every week. That is a great privilege in itself. Yet they still wake up one day and say, "That's all rubbish." That is what makes an apostate so culpable.

## Restoration Is Impossible

The flow of Hebrews **6:4-6** is as follows: "For it is impossible, in the case of those [who seemed like Christians] and then have fallen away, to restore them again to repentance."

There's a lot of debate about what this means. Is it really impossible for an apostate to come back again? Some **commentators** say that it is only impossible for men but not for God. Others say that it is impossible as long as the apostate refuses to repent. But many scholars simply state that it's genuinely impossible for a true apostate to come back.

What do we mean by that? There is a certain kind of rejection of God which leads to God giving a person over to their sin. This is a very scary idea, described in Romans 1:28. "Since they did not see fit to acknowledge God, God gave them up to a debased mind" (see also verses 24 and 26). People are so bent on their sin that God allows them to have their own way.

These verses are difficult and even frightening. However, there is hope. When we see someone leaving the covenant community, we don't know for certain that they are an apostate. Some people have periods of rebellion and resistance, and **church discipline** can bring them back in. We should always hope that that could happen when someone seems to be leaving the faith. It's the person who perseveres in their apostasy that proves they are a true apostate.

Our author goes on to say that apostates—those who persist in rejecting God and all the blessings he has given them—are basically crucifying Christ again. This is seen in the second half of Hebrews **6:6**: "They are crucifying once again the Son of God to their own harm and holding him up to contempt."

Of course, they are not literally crucifying Christ again. Christ only died once. But they are doing the same thing to Jesus as the people who crucified him. They are mocking him, rejecting him, and trying to humiliate him.

Apostates do this in the full knowledge of who Christ is. That is why they are subject to more severe judgment. It is not that if you've never heard the gospel, you're off the hook—no, all unbelievers will be accountable for their sin—but it is different to have received the gospel, heard good preaching, seen the Spirit at work, and then said no.

For example, imagine if you heard a news story about a young man killing an older couple in their eighties. You would no doubt think it was tragic. But if you found out that that young man was their son, whom they had lovingly raised, it would seem even more terrible. Murder is murder, of course; but when someone who has received blessing and love from another person rejects them and even takes their life, it is far worse. That is what apostasy is like.

Our author explains it with the analogy of land soaking up rain (**v 7-8**). When rain falls on land, it is supposed to produce crops. What if a piece of land soaks up a lot of rain but produces thistles instead of good crops? Is that land worth anything? No. In this analogy, the rain represents all the spiritual privileges and blessings described in **verses 4-5**. Don't be the land that responds to all that rain with thistles.

> This is a reminder to make sure that we own our faith for ourselves.

The implication to draw from all this is that spiritual privileges can't save. Someone might think that because they are a member of their church, they must be a true Christian. They may think that because they have been baptized, they are saved. They may think that enjoying worship on a Sunday morning is a sure sign of being saved. Some people trust in the fact that they grew up in a Christian home. But this warning is a reminder to each of us to make sure that we own our faith for ourselves and that we are not resting on any spiritual privileges as the basis for our salvation. We are saved through faith alone, in Christ alone.

## Signs of Salvation

Yet in **verse 9** the author gains a sense of optimism. "Though we speak in this way, yet in your case, beloved, we feel sure of better things—things that belong to salvation."

Despite being worried about their immaturity, the author does see some things that make him think that falling away will not be the fate of his readers. This is another reason why I think the prior passage is not describing true believers: because he goes on and says, *I don't think that's going to be you. I think that you really are saved.*

What is our author looking at that gives him optimism? There are three areas of fruitfulness that he mentions in **verse 10**: their labors in ministry ("your work"), their affection for God ("the love that you have shown for his name"), and their love for God's people ("serving the **saints**"). We can treat these three things as a litmus test for whether we are really saved, because together they express what it means to be Christ-like; and any Christian, no matter how long they have been a Christian, can participate in them at some level.

Where are you seeing fruit in your life right now? That question should both encourage you and challenge you—encourage you about the good fruit and challenge you about the areas where you need to grow. Every true believer produces fruit. There may not be all the fruit you want there to be, but there is fruit—some willingness to labor for God, some affection for his name, and some love for his people.

Finally, the author tells his readers that he wants them to press ahead in the future. Look at **verses 11-12**: "We desire each one of you to show the same earnestness to have the full assurance of hope until the end, so that you may not be sluggish, but imitators of those who through faith and patience inherit the promises."

This is forward-looking. He is giving them—and us—a little push, a little nudge down the right path.

First, be serious about faith—"show the same earnestness." I don't mean being serious in the sense of walking about with a scowl on your face. I mean taking your faith seriously: being earnest in it, being energetic about it, spending time over it.

Second, be hardworking, not "sluggish." Don't be lazy. We cannot work our way to heaven, but the Christian life is still labor. It's like the training of an athlete or a soldier. There is energy and hard work involved in it.

Third, have "patience." Someday, we are going to inherit the promises that the book of Hebrews talks about; but it will not happen overnight. It's a long haul. We need to have faith and patience.

In 2018 I watched the men's 15km cross-country skiing in the Winter Olympics. It is one of the most grueling, painful events of the whole games. The last man over the line was from Mexico—not a country that is big in skiing. Was he disappointed to come last? Not at all. He was elated just to finish the race. He carried a flag over the line while the crowds cheered. Some of the other competitors lifted him up on their shoulders to celebrate.

That is the vision in the Christian life. Personally, I'm not thinking about being the winner of the race. I just want to finish. That's the perseverance we are being called to. If apostasy is giving up alto-gether, then the opposite of apostasy is not getting a gold medal; it's finishing. Someday let us say with Paul, "I have finished the race" (2 Timothy 4:7).

## Questions for reflection

1. Why do you think God takes apostasy so seriously?

2. When you look at the fruit in your life, where are you encouraged that God is at work? Where are you discouraged?

3. What are some practical ways you can be "earnest" in faith in the year to come?

# 6. AN ANCHOR FOR OUR SOULS

A number of years ago, my wife, Melissa, and I went sailing with some friends in the British Virgin Islands. One day we were out on the sea and everything seemed to be fine—it was just a little overcast. But all of a sudden, out of nowhere, a storm rolled in, pulling us out into the ocean. The rain was coming down so hard that visibility was only about a hundred feet. Big waves were rocking the boat. Lightning was crashing around us. Then our GPS system shut down, and we no longer knew where we were. I really thought we were in big trouble.

Eventually the storm calmed down, and we made our way into the harbor. As we dropped anchor in the harbor, I remember thinking, "I hope it holds!" I did not want to wake up at one o'clock in the morning to find we were out again in the ocean. In weather like that, we needed something solid to hold us in position.

In Hebrews **6:19**, the writer speaks about "a sure and steadfast anchor of the soul." In the Christian life, you are going to get beaten around by waves. It can feel like you are about to be pulled away by the currents—things that make you doubt God. That might be pain in your life and the lives of others, or terrible news stories, or hostility from unbelievers, or something else. What you need more than anything, if you are going to hold to your faith, is an anchor. And we have one. This is what the writer to the Hebrews wants to remind us of. He encourages us with the truth that we can trust God because of Jesus.

In **6:13-19** our author uses the example of the promise God made to Abraham to assure us that we can trust God's promise to us. Then **6:20** leads us into chapter 7, where our author explains more about why we can trust Jesus above all.

## Doubting God's Promises

Think about the promises God has made to you in his word. He has promised to meet your needs (Luke 12:22-31). He has promised to hear your prayers (Matthew 7:7-11). He has promised never to forsake you or leave you (Hebrews 13:5). He has promised to forgive you of your sins if you trust in Christ (Ephesians 1:7). He has promised to strengthen you and to dwell within you by his Holy Spirit (Ephesians 3:16). He has promised one day to bring you into glory (Colossians 3:4).

But so often there remains a tickle of doubt in the back of the mind.

Our author knows that and pulls in the story of Abraham as an example of trusting God when it is hard to do so.

In Hebrews **6:13-14** the author is pointing the reader back to Genesis 22:16-17. This is the chapter in which God told Abraham to sacrifice his son, Isaac, on Mount Moriah. Abraham obeyed and was right at the point of sacrificing his son when God stopped him and provided a ram to take Isaac's place. It is a picture of how God provides a substitute for our sins.

Imagine the anguish that Abraham must have felt at the moment when God gave him that command! It was not just that Abraham loved his son and did not want to lose him. It was that God had promised Abraham several times that he was going to give him descendants and fill the earth with them (Genesis 12:2; 13:16; 15:5; 17:4; 18:18). Abraham and his wife Sarah had waited and waited, and finally they had had a son, Isaac—the key to God's promise. Abraham must have wondered how God could keep his promise to give him many descendants if he took his son's life.

We have the same kinds of doubts. Is God really going to keep his promises? Maybe you doubt that you are really saved. Maybe you doubt God's goodness. Maybe you doubt that God really loves you. Maybe you doubt that there is really life after death.

How can we persevere in the midst of such doubts? We can use Abraham as an example. Remember that Abraham did not see the realization of God's promise straight away. He "patiently waited" (Hebrews **6:15**). God does things on his own timetable, not ours; and he often uses means that we do not expect. That can make us start to doubt. But we need to follow Abraham's example and wait patiently, obediently, and peaceably.

Yet, second, we can also actively fight our doubts. The Christian life should be one of assurance because we are certain about who God is. The Christian church should not be a place where people cannot express their doubts and concerns; but nor should we act as if doubt is all there is. The Bible reassures us that we can trust God. This is what enables us to persevere.

God reassures us here in Hebrews **6:13-20** that we have great reasons to trust his promises. There are three strands in the anchor rope: God's oath, God's character, and God's Son.

## Trusting God's Oath

God had already promised Abraham that he would bless and multiply him, but he reinforced that promise by swearing an oath. In **verse 13** we hear that God "swore by himself." This is further explained in **verse 16**: "For people swear by something greater than themselves, and in all their disputes an oath is final for confirmation."

In a court of law, when you are about to give a testimony, you put your hand on the Bible and swear to tell the truth, the whole truth, and nothing but the truth, and add "So help me God." You are promising that what you are about to say is trustworthy because you are swearing on a higher power.

If we swear by God when we make an oath, what can God himself swear by? There is nothing and no one higher than him. That is why "he swore by himself." God is the guarantor of his own promises because he is the very highest authority.

Remember, God did not *need* to swear an oath. His promises are always true. But he swore an oath to Abraham in order to help him. He recognizes how weak we are—how many doubts we have—and he gives us an extra layer of assurance. He swore this oath "to show more convincingly … the unchangeable character of his purpose" (**v 17**). God's oath is an act of grace—not because his word is in doubt but because *we* are in doubt.

But this oath was not just to reassure Abraham. God wanted to convince "the heirs of the promise."

As surprising as it may be, the oath that God swore to Abraham is partly about *you*. "If you are Christ's, then you are Abraham's off-spring, heirs according to promise" (Galatians 3:29; see also Romans 4:11-12, 16-17). In Christ, you are part of God's promise to bless the nations through Abraham's family. And if Abraham "obtained the promise" (Hebrews **6:15**), you will too.

## Trusting God's Character

The second of our three strands is God's character. This is closely related to his oath. God has sworn an oath on himself; we can trust that oath because we know who God is.

When a person makes a promise to you, why do you believe it? Probably because you know that person: you've spent time with them, and you trust them. You know they are honest and reliable. The same goes for trusting God.

In **verses 17-18** our author points out that you can be sure of God's promises, not only because he swears by them but also because of the nature of God himself.

First, God desired to show "the unchangeable character of his purpose" (**v 17**). This tells you something about the way God is. His purpose doesn't change. He doesn't back out of things. Second, "it is impossible for God to lie" (**v 18**). God does not say one thing and then do another. He does not deceive us.

Why was Abraham willing to sacrifice his son? Genesis doesn't tell us what was going through his mind, but the book of Hebrews does, later on in 11:19: "He considered that God was able even to raise him from the dead." Abraham was so sure that God would keep his promises—so sure that God would bless his offspring—that he believed that if he took Isaac's life, God would raise him from the dead. How amazing is that confidence? Abraham had absolute assurance that God would keep his promises; he knew that he was the kind of God who could even raise people from the dead.

If we lack this kind of confidence in God's character, there are plenty of ways to build it again. We could look back at our own lives and the good track record he has with us. We should certainly read the Bible, which contains the history of how God has dealt with his people over thousands and thousands of years; it will help us understand and trust God's character. We can also read good books on theology to help us to understand God better. And we need to spend time with him in prayer, investing in a **devotional life** in order to build confidence that God is the kind of God who delivers on his promises.

## Trusting God's Son

These "two unchangeable things"—God's oath and God's character—give us "strong encouragement to hold fast to the hope set before us" (**6:18**). But in **verses 19-20** we learn that there is also a third strand to the anchor rope: God's Son.

> "We have this as a sure and steadfast anchor of the soul, a hope that enters into the inner place behind the curtain, where Jesus has gone as a forerunner on our behalf."

Why should you be confident that God is going to keep his promises? Because of what Jesus has done. That is the essence of this anchor of the soul.

Jesus has gone "behind the curtain" (**v 19**). The curtain is what you would have seen if you had gone to worship at the temple in the first century. The Most Holy Place, where God's presence dwelt, was blocked off by a huge curtain. It sent a clear theological message: God is holy and as a sinful person you cannot have access to him.

But Jesus has actually gone behind the curtain, so to speak. He acted as our great high priest. He has gone into the heavenly Most Holy Place "as a forerunner on our behalf" (**v 20**). That means that the work of Christ paved the way for us so that we too can have access to God. When Jesus died on the cross, that temple curtain was ripped in half (Matthew 27:51). This happened in order to show that we now have access to God and intimate fellowship with him. That was God's whole purpose in sending his Son. What greater reassurance that God keeps his promises do you need?

> When the storms come, instead of looking around or inward, we need to look forward to the day when we will be with Christ.

Anchors typically go down. But this anchor of the soul goes up. It is an anchor in heaven for you to hold onto. If you are in Christ, you have a place there that will never be taken away. This is the hope set before us, to which we must hold fast (Hebrews **6:18**).

We can trust God because of his oath, because of his character, and because of his Son. These assurances are all external to us—they do not depend on us but are **objectively** real outside of us. Even if you are full of doubts, you can trust the truth of who God is and what Jesus has done. When the storms come, instead of looking around at our problems or inward at ourselves, we need to look forward to the day when we will be with Christ.

## The Order of Melchizedek

But **verse 20** doesn't stop there. Our author adds one more phrase. Jesus entered the Most Holy Place on our behalf, "having become a high priest for ever after the order of Melchizedek."

Melchizedek has been mentioned briefly before (5:6, 10), but this still feels like a curveball. Who is Melchizedek? And what does he have to do with our confidence in Christ? The first few verses of chapter 7 begin the explanation.

In Genesis 14, Abraham was coming back from a battle. His nephew Lot had been taken captive; Abraham and his men had pursued the captors, defeated them, and brought back Lot along with the spoils of victory (Genesis 14:8-16). On the way back, he met Melchizedek (14:18-20) and gave him a tenth part of all the spoils.

Melchizedek is a historical figure, a real person. But, more importantly, he is also a type of Christ—a figure who points forward to Jesus and what he would do. Such historical figures, events, and institutions in the Old Testament were set up by God intentionally to point forward to the coming Savior and let people know what he would be like.

Melchizedek was "the king of Salem" (Hebrews **7:1**). This means that he was actually the king of Jerusalem: Salem would become Jerusalem. But he was also the "priest of the Most High God." Melchizedek was both king and priest at the same time. No other figure in the Bible ever held both offices—until Jesus.

In **6:20** our author quotes Psalm 110:4 and tells us that it is about Jesus. The person addressed as "a priest ... after the order of Melchizedek" is a king (as verses 1-2 of the psalm reveal). So being "after the order of Melchizedek" means being like Melchizedek—being both priest and king. Psalm 110 predicted such a figure: the coming Messiah.

Melchizedek's name and title also point to Jesus (Hebrews **7:2**). The name "Melchizedek" literally means "king of righteousness." *Salem* is a variant of the word *shalom*, which means peace. So, he is also a "king of peace." Both phrases describe Jesus (see Isaiah 9:6; 11:4).

Hebrews **7:3** tells us that Melchizedek resembled Jesus in another way: he seemed eternal. "He is without father or mother or genealogy, having neither beginning of days nor end of life, but resembling the Son of God he continues a priest forever."

What does that mean? Was he an angel, not a human being? Was he a vision of Christ himself?

No, it seems that Melchizedek was a real human, and thus would have had a real father and mother. But the way that Melchizedek is *presented* in Scripture makes it seem that he pops in and pops out without a beginning or an end. He shows up on the scene out of nowhere and then disappears. We are not told anything about his parents nor where he comes from. So, he seems eternal. Therefore, he is a very effective type of Christ: "resembling the Son of God."

Why does all this matter? Why bring Melchizedek up? It is to show that Christ's priesthood is superior to the Old Testament Levitical priesthood—and that should give us confidence.

Maybe that explanation just gives you more questions! But stepping through the remainder of Hebrews 7 will help us to understand more.

## Questions for reflection

1. In what ways do you see people struggling to trust God and his word today? What about you personally? How does this passage help to reassure you?

2. How are you doing today in terms of waiting patiently on the Lord? What would it look like in the week ahead for you to do this?

3. How does the Melchizedek passage remind you of the importance of noticing every detail in the text? How does it reassure you that the Bible is a divinely authored book?

## PART TWO

### Two Priesthoods

When we think of priests in the Bible, we are generally thinking of the Levitical priesthood. Levites were the descendants of Levi, one of **Jacob**'s twelve sons. When the Israelites had conquered the promised land, the Levites were not given a portion of the land like the other tribes. Instead their job was to work in the temple—handling all the details and logistics of temple life. A subset of the Levites—those who were descended from Aaron, the brother of Moses—could become priests.

But our passage introduces another priesthood: one in the order of Melchizedek, who lived long before Levi and Aaron. And our author is going to make a very simple argument: *Melchizedek's priestly order is greater than the Levitical priesthood.* Why would that matter? Because Christ is "after the order of Melchizedek" (**6:20**). That means that Christ's priesthood is what we are talking about when we refer to Melchizedek's priesthood. Christ's priesthood is better than the Levitical priesthood.

This argument is part of the larger theme of the book: namely, that Christ is superior to all aspects of the old covenant—he's better than angels, Moses, Joshua, and even the Levitical priesthood.

In **7:4-10**, our author makes three arguments for the superiority of Melchizedek's priesthood over the Levitical priesthood. First, Abraham gave **tithes** to Melchizedek: "See how great this man was to whom Abraham the **patriarch** gave a tenth of the spoils" (**v 4**).

In **verse 5** our author describes the usual tithing system: the priests "have a commandment in the law to take tithes from the people." The point is that normally the Levites were *given* tithes. Because Levitical priests did not have their own land, they received tithes—ten percent of income—from everybody who came to worship. It was a kind of salary.

But in this instance with Melchizedek, things were very different. For one, tithes were being paid to someone "who does not have his descent from [the Levites]" (**v 6**). Melchizedek was not receiving a tithe for the normal reasons a priest might receive a tithe—he was not a Levite. Instead he was receiving a tithe because of how special he was.

On top of this, it was effectively the Levites who were giving the tithe to Melchizedek: "Levi himself, who [normally] receives tithes, paid tithes through Abraham, for he was still in the **loins** of his ancestor" (**v 9-10**). Think about how incredible this would be. The Levites (through Abraham) were not getting a tithe but paying one! It's an amazing reversal.

So then, the order of Melchizedek had to be superior to the Levitical priesthood. And who is in the order of Melchizedek? Jesus. The simple point of all this detail about tithing is that Christ is superior to any ordinary priest.

The second reason why we know that Melchizedek's priesthood is superior to the Levitical one is because it is *eternal*. In **verse 8** we are reminded that in ancient Israel tithes were received by "mortal men" (the Levites), whereas in the case of Melchizedek tithes were received "by one of whom it is testified that he lives."

This theme of the eternality of Christ's priesthood has already come up earlier (5:6), and will even come up again later in this chapter (**7:16-17**). But it is so important that our author mentions it again here. Which priesthood would you rather have representing you? One in which the priests die and always have to be replaced? Or one in which you have an intercessor that lives forever to represent you?

Only Melchizedek's priesthood—the priesthood of Christ—is everlasting.

The third reason why Melchizedek's priesthood is superior is because Melchizedek was superior to Abraham. How do we know this? Because Melchizedek "blessed him (Abraham) who had the promises" (**v 6**). For the Jewish people, Abraham was the most revered of figures. As the original recipient of God's promises, he was the one that everything went back to. To be blessed by Israel's patriarch would therefore be the highest of honors.

But that is precisely what makes this scene so remarkable. It is not Abraham who blesses Melchizedek but Melchizedek who blesses Abraham! Our author explains why this is significant: "It is beyond dispute that the inferior is blessed by the superior" (**v 7**). Incredibly, there is someone greater than Abraham here: Melchizedek.

And if Melchizedek is greater than Abraham, then Jesus must be greater than Abraham—and thus greater than Abraham's descendants, the Levites. Once again, this is an argument for why Christ's priesthood is superior to the Levitical priesthood.

## A Change in the Priesthood

But our author is not finished. In **verses 13-28** he mounts an even fuller case for the superiority of Christ's priesthood, laying out four additional reasons why we should always turn to Christ as our true high priest.

Before we dive into those four reasons, notice that this section begins with a general observation about *why* we need a new or different priesthood: the Levitical priesthood was unable to attain "perfection" (**v 11**). In other words, the Old Testament priesthood was unable to *really* cleanse God's people from their sins and make them fit to dwell with God forever (see 10:1).

This verse highlights a central theme in the book of Hebrews, one which will be revisited again in the next three chapters: namely, that the old-covenant infrastructure was inadequate and temporary and would soon be replaced by a "better" covenant (**7:22**). This doesn't mean, of course, that the old covenant was sinful or wrong. No, it was simply *provisional*, pointing forward to the One who would ultimately achieve redemption for us: Jesus Christ.

As for the need for a new priesthood, our author indicates that we should have seen that coming. Remember, Psalm 110:4 promised there would be a new priesthood in the order of Melchizedek—a passage alluded to already (Hebrews 5:6; 6:20). If the first priesthood had been just fine, argues our author, then "what further need would there have been for another priest to arise after the order of Melchizedek?" (**7:11**).

But if there's a change in the priesthood, "there is necessarily a change in the law as well" (**v 12**). You see, the Levitical priesthood was part of the law of Moses, given to the Israelites at Mount Sinai. The priesthood and the law were intertwined in such a way that **verse 11** can say: "... for under it [that is, the priesthood] the people received the law."

Therefore, the change in priesthood implies a larger change in the law. Put differently, a change in priesthood implies there will be a *new covenant* that will supersede the old—a theme our author will revisit in chapter 8.

Now that our author has addressed the reason for a new priesthood, he turns to the four features of Christ's priesthood that make it superior.

## Jesus Is From a Better Tribe

First, "the one of whom these things are spoken belonged to another tribe, from which no one has ever served at the altar. For it is evident that our Lord was descended from **Judah**, and in connection with that tribe Moses said nothing about priests" (**7:13-14**).

> Jesus is like no other priest— he is a priest who can also rule as king.

It may seem pedantic to argue about which tribe you come from. But it was important in Old Testament Israel. Priests could normally only come from the tribe of Levi, but Jesus was a descendant of Judah, the tribe of kings (Genesis 49:10).

Why does this matter? Because it means that *Jesus could be both priest and king* at the same time. This was essential because the

Messiah was predicted to hold both offices: "There shall be a priest on his throne ... And the crown shall be in the temple of the LORD" (Zechariah 6:13-14).

The significance of this becomes clear when you consider how rigidly the two offices were separated in the Old Testament. Recall the story of King **Saul** on the eve of battle with the **Philistines**, waiting for **Samuel** to come and offer a sacrifice. When Samuel doesn't show up, Saul decides to offer the sacrifices himself. When Samuel arrives, he is very displeased, saying, "What have you done?" (1 Samuel 13:11). It is not acceptable for the king to make a sacrifice. In short, kings and priests are different offices.

But not when it comes to Jesus. Jesus is like no other priest in the Old Testament—he is a priest who can also rule as king. He cannot only save us (as a priest); he can care for us and protect us (as a king).

## Jesus Intercedes Forever

The coming of Jesus makes it "even more evident" (Hebrews **7:15**) that there has been a monumental change in the priesthood; and one of those changes is that this new priest will never die. Jesus' priesthood is not based on "bodily descent" (**v 16**) from Levi but on the fact that he has an "indestructible life" and therefore will never need another priest to succeed him. Our author provides proof for this point by quoting again from Psalm 110:4. "You are a priest forever, after the order of Melchizedek" (Hebrews **7:17**).

Here we come to the second thing that makes Christ's priesthood superior: namely, that he *lives forever*. As we noted above, this theme has cropped up already (5:6; 7:8).

In **verses 23-25**, our author expands on why the eternal nature of Christ's priesthood matters so much. In Old Testament times, every priest was temporary. He would be there for a little while, and then he would be gone because "they were prevented by death from continuing in office" (**v 23**).

Most people in ancient Israel may not even have put two and two together regarding the problem presented by the priestly system and the fact that priests would die. If the person you are relying on to intercede for you will die, that means the effectiveness of the intercession has some uncertainty. How could we have eternal security without an eternal representative?

But when it comes to Jesus, you don't have to worry about that. He has no successor because he never dies. "He holds his priesthood permanently" (**v 24**). That means that Jesus, as the eternal high priest, is able to provide that eternal security which we need: "Consequently, he is able to save to the uttermost those who draw near to God through him, since he always lives to make intercession for them" (**v 25**).

Jesus, unlike any other priest, will always, always, always be there for you. Eternity is a scary thing, but in Jesus we can rest secure.

In the middle of this section about the eternal nature of Christ's intercession come **verses 18-19**, where our author takes the opportunity to speak about the contrast between the two priesthoods. He reminds us once more that the Levitical priesthood—what he calls the "former commandment"—has been "set aside because of its weakness and uselessness" (**v 18**).

Why exactly was it useless? Because "the law made nothing perfect" (**v 19**). The author returns here to the theme of **verse 11**: namely, that the Levitical system, with the shedding of the blood of animals, could never really take away sins. It could never make a person "perfect" and able to enter God's holy presence.

But there's good news. In Christ, "a better hope is introduced, through which we draw near to God" (**v 19**). To say we have a "better hope" is not to say that we are more hopeful people, as if it referred to our **subjective** feelings. Rather a "better hope" refers to the objective character or quality of the thing we are trusting in. We are trusting in something better than the Levitical priesthood. We are trusting in

Jesus, who allows us to really "draw near to God"—something the old priesthood could never do.

To say Jesus is "better" essentially captures the theme of the entire book of Hebrews, and it will come up again: Jesus brings a "better covenant" (**7:22**; 8:6); "better promises" (8:6); "better sacrifices" (9:23); and a "better country—that is, a heavenly one" (11:16).

## Jesus' Priesthood Is Certain

Since our author has just discussed this radical change in the priesthood (**7:18-19**), he knows there may be a concern brewing in the minds of his readers. How do we know that God won't change the priesthood again in the future? How do we know that Jesus' new priestly order won't be retracted just like the last one?

In order to reassure us, the author points out a third feature of Jesus' priesthood, namely that it "was not without an oath" (**v 20**). When did God swear this oath? Our author cites a new portion of Psalm 110:4: "The Lord has sworn and will not change his mind, 'You are a priest forever'" (Hebrews **7:21**).

> God is not changing his mind on this. He will never back out.

This is a remarkable feature of Christ's priesthood. Essentially, God swore that he would not change his mind this time around. Christ's priesthood is certain. This oath makes Jesus the "guarantor of a better covenant" (**v 22**). Unlike the old-covenant arrangement, this new priesthood is guaranteed forever.

In contrast, "those who formerly became priests were made such without an oath" (**v 20**). God never said, *I promise you, Aaron will be my priest forever.* He never said, *I swear that the earthly temple system is the way it's going to be forever.* But when he gets to Jesus, he swears an oath.

We talked about oaths already in discussing 6:13-18. God never breaks his promises, and when he swears an oath, he is giving us an extra degree of assurance. Jesus will always be your high priest. God is not changing his mind on this one. He will never back out. Jesus will always be there, interceding for us. Who else in the whole world could ever be that kind of savior? No one.

## Jesus Is a Perfect Priest

This leads us to the final—and perhaps the ultimate—feature of Jesus' priesthood. Unlike any other priest in history, Jesus is sinless. His priesthood is different because he is perfect: "holy, innocent, unstained, separated from sinners, and exalted above the heavens" (**7:26**).

Why does this matter? For one, Jesus did not have to offer sacrifices "for his own sins" (**v 27**) as the Old Testament priests did. And more importantly, Jesus' perfect, sinless life allowed him to do something unthinkable—something no other priest would have ever dreamed of doing: he "offered up himself."

In this way, Jesus is the perfect fulfillment of all the animal sacrifices of the Old Testament. When a priest chose an animal to sacrifice, it had to be perfect—without spot or blemish. It could not be crippled or sick because it was symbolically representing the innocent party that would die in place of the guilty. The guilty cannot die for the guilty. Only the innocent can do that.

So our author ends with one final contrast between the two priestly systems. On the one hand, "the **law** appoints men in their weakness," but on the other we have "a Son who has been made perfect forever" (**v 28**). The contrast could not be greater.

And within that contrast is the heart of the gospel. We are broken, sinful people who are separated from the holy God, and no ordinary priest, no earthly system, no animal sacrifice is enough to bridge that gap. What we need is the perfect Son of God, who became a human being, to represent us before God as our great high priest forever.

Because of his perfect obedience and his indestructible life, we can have great confidence that our sins are forgiven, and therefore that we can "draw near" to God with confidence.

With such a Savior available to us, why turn to anything else? Whatever we are tempted to trust in today other than Jesus, the book of Hebrews bids us to let it go. Only Jesus is sufficient to save. Only he is worthy of our hope and trust.

## Questions for reflection

1. Do you feel that you read the Old Testament as if it is really about Christ? How does this passage help you to do that better?

2. Do you ever struggle with doubts about whether the work of Jesus is really able to save you? How does this passage provide reassurance?

3. How do both Jesus' life and his death work together to save us?

# 7. A BETTER COVENANT

"Are we okay?" "Are we good?"

People suffer a tremendous amount of anxiety over difficult human relationships. We worry about them a lot. We ask each other, "Are we okay?" What we mean is: "Is there something that needs fixing and repairing here?"

But most people rarely think about asking those questions in regard to God. In fact, many people skip through life thinking that God is pretty pleased with them. It doesn't dawn on them for a moment that their relationship with God might actually be broken.

The biblical story is that every human being is born a sinful person, estranged from God. So, if anyone goes to God on their own merits and asks, "Are we okay?" the answer will be "No, we're not okay." God is holy, and we are sinful. The relationship is broken, and we cannot do anything (on our own) to fix it.

In Hebrews 8 – 10, we see very clearly that there is a better way for us to fix our relationship with God. Our author has already discussed how Jesus is a better priest than any previous priest. He now develops that by describing how Jesus brings in a whole new way of relating to God. By comparing the old covenant under Moses with the new covenant in Christ, he shows that the law and the sacrificial system were always intended to point to Jesus.

Now, this doesn't mean that people weren't saved by Jesus under the old covenant. They were saved in the same way as we are saved now: by faith alone in the sacrificial work of Christ alone. They looked ahead to Christ—through the **types** and shadows of the sacrificial system—and we look back to Christ. While the blood of bulls and goats does not, in and of itself, take away sins (Hebrews 10:4), it does point toward the thing that does: the sacrifice of Christ.

Hebrews 8 starts off this section of the book by introducing the new covenant brought in by Jesus—which is far better than the old system under Moses.

## The True Tent

**Verses 1-6** describe the old-covenant sacrificial system and how it pointed to Jesus. We see what the old-covenant priests did and how Jesus, in the new covenant, provides a superior priesthood.

Our author begins with the unique location of Jesus' ministry: he is "one who is seated at the right hand of the throne of the majesty in heaven" (**v 1**). This is an allusion to Psalm 110:1, where the Messiah is given a place of honor and glory at the right hand of God.

It is significant that Jesus is "a **minister** in the holy places, the true tent that the Lord set up, not man" (Hebrews **8:2**). Jesus does his work of mediation in heaven in the very presence of God himself.

This stands as a contrast to the high priest in the old covenant. On the Day of Atonement, after offering sacrifices, he would take the blood inside the earthly "tent" known as the tabernacle and sprinkle it on the ark of the covenant in the innermost chamber known as the "Most Holy Place" (or the "Holy of Holies").

God himself gave very particular instructions to Moses about this tent: "See that you make everything according to the pattern that was shown you on the mountain" (**v 5**). But we are told—and this is the key—that this earthly tent was merely "a copy and shadow" of the heavenly tabernacle.

This means that the tabernacle was simply a man-made tent that was symbolic of the real dwelling place of God in heaven. Sure, God did dwell in the earthly tabernacle in a sense. But God's real dwelling place is in heaven itself. This is the better temple which Jesus entered.

So, Jesus' priesthood is superior precisely because of *where* his ministry takes place. Christ's sacrifice is presented in the "true tent" of heaven itself, in the very presence of God.

## A Better Ministry

The second unique feature of Jesus' priesthood pertains to the sacrifice that Jesus offered. Like any priest, Jesus would have been expected to bring a sacrifice: "Every high priest is appointed to offer gifts and sacrifices; thus it is necessary for this priest [Jesus] also to have something to offer" (**v 3**).

But we wouldn't expect Jesus to bring an ordinary sacrifice. Why? Because he's not an ordinary priest. In fact, our author goes out of his way to remind us of this fact: "If he were on earth, he would not be a priest at all" (**v 4**). Our author is not denying that part of Jesus' redemptive activity took place on earth. Rather, he's emphasizing that Jesus did not operate like the Levitical priests; he never entered the earthly temple in Jerusalem as they did.

This fact is worth pausing on for a moment. Have you ever noticed that Jesus never even tried to enter the Holy of Holies to be in God's presence? As the Son of God, he would have had as much right to be there as anyone. But that was not the nature of his priesthood. He knew his priestly ministry was going to be in heaven, not on earth.

Because Jesus' priesthood is different, we would expect his sacrifice to be different. The priests made offerings "according to the law," but not Jesus. No, he offered what no other priest in the history of Israel had ever done: he offered *himself*.

And there is no sacrifice that can put you in better stead with God than Jesus. In fact, he is the only one who can put you in good stead with God. That is what we saw in 7:26-27: he offered himself as a perfect sacrifice and dealt with our sin once and for all.

Little wonder that, in **8:6**, our author sums it up by saying that Christ's ministry is "much more excellent" than the old ministry of the priests. And if Christ is better, then "the covenant he **mediates** is better."

## Understanding Covenants

When two people get married, they stand in front of a congregation and make promises to one another. They enter into an agreement—like a contract. They also exchange signs of that agreement: rings which they wear for the rest of their lives to remind them of the promises they have made. What they are doing is entering into a covenant. A covenant is simply an arrangement in which two parties make vows to one another and exchange symbols associated with those promises. People can make covenants with one another. But God also enters into covenants.

God has always saved his people through what theologians call the covenant of **grace**, which was revealed in stages. God first made a covenant with Abraham, promising that he would be his God and would establish his family (Genesis 15). Much later, he made a covenant with Abraham's descendants, the people of Israel, after he delivered them from slavery in Egypt (Exodus 24:3-8).

This was like God getting married. He was the groom, and Israel was his bride; promises were exchanged, vows were made, and signs were given. But then God's bride ran off with other gods. The Israelites did not keep their promises.

Unlike many human husbands, God did not end it there. He said, *I am going to pursue my people again.* He promised a new covenant.

## The Need for a New Covenant

In Hebrews **8:8-12** our author quotes from Jeremiah 31:31-34:

"Behold, the days are coming, declares the Lord, when I will establish a new covenant with the house of Israel and the house of Judah." (Hebrews **8:8**)

In the time of Jeremiah, things in Israel were an utter shambles. The nation was divided into two kingdoms. Exile was on the horizon. Idolatry was rampant. Things had fallen apart. The few people who really loved God were desperate for him to do something. So, God stepped onto the scene in Jeremiah 31 and said, *I will*. He would renew his covenant and go after his bride again. He would come and set things right.

God does not say that he is going to make a new covenant with a new set of people. The nucleus remains "the house of Israel and the house of Judah." So, if you are part of the new covenant, you're part of the new Israel. Romans 11:17 explains that the Gentiles (non-Israelites) have been "grafted in" to the tree of Abraham—a new branch becoming part of the old plant.

By "Israel" we no longer mean a physical, political entity but a spiritual reality. But there is clear continuity. God does not abandon his people and start again with a completely different set. He renews and expands his people in the promises of Christ.

Our author mentions two reasons why a new covenant was needed. First is that the old covenant was faulty. He reminds us, "If that first covenant had been faultless there would have been no occasion to look for a second" (Hebrews **8:7**). Saying that the old covenant was faulty does not mean that it was wrong or sinful or bad. It simply means that it could not accomplish what it looked forward to. It was provisional. Indeed, this was the point in chapter 7: the old covenant priesthood was not able to provide "perfection" (7:11).

The second problem with the old covenant was that the *people* were faulty. In **8:8** our author says that "[God] finds fault with them"—not with "it" but with "them": that is, with Old Testament Israel. We see this more fully in **verse 9**: "They did not continue in my covenant."

The problem with the old-covenant people was simply that they broke their covenant. They were idolaters. Like a cheating spouse, they ran off with other gods.

The God of heaven had gone to the people of Israel, his bride, and given everything to her—loving her and pledging himself to her. He "took them by the hand" (**v 9**). Yet off Israel went.

But such is the heart of God that he pursues even those who wander and flee.

God is an unrelenting pursuer of those he loves. He will not stop. He will not quit. He will not cease. He even goes to his own death in Jesus Christ to win his bride. Yet you and I still say, "I'm not sure you really love me!" We all struggle with doubt, but this is the cure: to realize that you have a God who has gone every extra mile—who has given more grace than is imaginable—to pursue a wayward bride. That kind of God is not going to abandon us.

## New-Covenant Glories

The old covenant had been abandoned by Israel, and so God established a new covenant. There were three things that were new about this new covenant: it involved new power, new people, and a new priest.

As we enter into this comparison between the old and new covenants, we need to begin by remembering that the contrast between them is not absolute. We must be careful not to overstate the differences in a way that caricatures the old covenant as harsh, cold, legalistic, and only concerned with externals. Nor should we present the new covenant as unconcerned with the law or with obedience. As we shall see, the differences between the covenants are often a matter of degree.

To be sure, the old covenant had a lot of externals. It involved rituals and laws. But these external things were always meant to be a sign of what was going on inside—of the love and faith that people should have had for God in their hearts. And many Israelites did love God from the heart (1 Samuel 13:14; 2 Kings 23:25; Psalm 40:8; Acts 13:22).

However, much of Israel was simply laboring to keep the law and perform the rituals, without stopping to think about their meaning. Their religion became a largely external matter with no internal dimension—no heart.

We tend to like external performance because it is measurable. Boxes can be checked and then compared to other people's, and we can feel good about ourselves. We feel as though we are in control of our own fates. That is what our sinful selves want.

But I can tell you this: if you try to keep God's law merely as an external thing with no real heart in it, you will have a difficult time. You will turn into a Pharisee, cracking the whip to get everyone to obey.

> Now you are empowered to obey God.

But the new covenant would involve something different:

"This is the covenant that I will make with the house of Israel after those days, declares the Lord: I will put my laws into their minds, and write them on their hearts ... they shall all know me, from the least of them to the greatest." (Hebrews **8:10-11**)

God was going to provide *new power* for his people. He was going to write his law on their hearts. He would pour out his Holy Spirit and change them from the inside.

The new covenant still involves law-keeping. God still cares about obedience. The difference is in how you obey him. In the new covenant, the Holy Spirit is poured out in greater measure on every one of God's people (Romans 5:5; 1 Corinthians 12:13). Now you are empowered to obey God in the way you always should have done.

The new covenant also involves a *new people*. There were many people in the nation of Israel under the old covenant who performed the rituals and kept the law but who did not really believe. So, the people of Israel were often told, "Know the Lord" (**v 11**). But under the new covenant, due to the pouring out of the Holy Spirit, there is essentially a **revival**. "For they shall all know me, from the least of them to the greatest."

Of course, we should remember that this new-covenant promise is not fully realized in the present—we should not expect a completely pure church now. As the book of Hebrews itself shows, there are still unbelievers within the new covenant community. In fact, the whole theme of apostasy shows that people can be part of the covenant community and yet still "fall away" (Hebrews 10:29). But one day these new covenant promises will be realized completely, when Christ returns and the church is made pure.

Third, there is a *new priest*. God promised, "I will be merciful towards their iniquities, and I will remember their sins no more" (**8:12**). How is that possible? Because—as the writer to the Hebrews has repeatedly told us—we have a priest who enables sins to be fully and finally forgiven.

To be clear, sins were forgiven in Old Testament times too. But they were forgiven in anticipation of Christ's forthcoming work. The blood of bulls and goats, in and of itself, could never accomplish forgiveness (Hebrews 10:4). In the new covenant, that forgiveness has been fully achieved.

"I will remember their sins no more." Have you ever had the experience of someone continually bringing up something you did in the past? You regretted it and apologized and you thought it was done with, but the person keeps throwing it back in your face. The forgiveness we have in Christ is far deeper than that. God promises to completely forget our sins—not because he does not care about sin but because Jesus is enough to cover it.

These are the reasons why the new covenant is so much better. The old covenant was good, but God made it "obsolete" when he spoke of a new covenant (**8:13**). Jesus has gloriously fulfilled all that the old covenant pointed to.

## Questions for reflection

1.  In what ways do you still struggle with keeping God's law only on an external basis? How does this passage help you?

2.  How does the new covenant actually make us (perhaps unexpectedly) better law-keepers? What does that say about the role of grace in our lives?

3.  How does God's persistent pursuit of his wayward people encourage you today?

## PART TWO

### The Limitations of the Old Covenant

When I was growing up, my favorite film was *Raiders of the Lost Ark*. It features Harrison Ford in his prime as the archaeologist Indiana Jones. Really, though, the star of the show was not Indiana Jones but what he finds in the movie: the ark of the covenant. This was a golden box which represented God's holy presence.

The God of the ark of the covenant is not a God you cozy up to easily. In the movie, when the explorers open the lid, they are killed by the fire of God's holiness. Eventually the ark is hidden away in a crate in some warehouse, because everyone is afraid of it. The message is: *God is holy, so leave him well alone.*

*Raiders of the Lost Ark* is just a movie, and it is filled with Hollywood speculation about what the ark would be like. But what the movie does get right is that God is more holy than you can possibly imagine. You cannot just charge into his presence.

The idea that God is holy and at a distance encapsulates the experience of Old Testament worshipers. They took part in real worship, and it was the real God they were worshiping; but it all had to be done at a distance. Access was denied.

Hebrews **9:1-10** highlights these sorts of limitations of old-covenant worship. It accomplishes this by taking the reader deep into the inner workings of the tabernacle. What was in the tabernacle? What did you experience there and what did you do? The old-covenant worship was ordained by God, and therefore it was good. But it had all kinds of limitations to it.

Throughout these verses, the author's point is simple: *Don't you want to worship God in a way that involves full access? That is what Jesus makes possible.*

## An Earthly Place

**Verses 1-5** describe the tabernacle: the "earthly place of holiness" (**v 1**), where people under the old covenant tried to approach God. This had a larger courtyard with a fence around it, where sacrifices took place, but the tabernacle proper was "a tent" (**v 2**) with two sections.

The first section, the "Holy Place," held the lampstand, the table, and the bread of the Presence.

You will have seen pictures of this lampstand: it was a menorah, with seven branches, each one with a cup-shaped oil lamp at the top (Exodus 25:31-40). One of the jobs of a priest was to make sure that the light never went out during the night (Exodus 27:21). The bread of the Presence was actually twelve loaves (Leviticus 24:5-9). These loaves were baked fresh every week; once the new loaves were in place, the priests would consume the old loaves. There was always bread there, but it had to be continually replaced.

Both the lampstand and the bread point to Christ. Jesus identifies himself as the light of the world (John 9:5) and the bread of life (John 6:35). Not only is he the new temple (John 2:21); he is the new bread of the Presence—which never has to be replaced. By "eating" this bread—by putting our trust in his broken body—all believers enjoy access to the holy places.

The first section of the temple contained these pointers toward Christ. Yet only the priest could go in there. Other worshipers had to remain outside in the courtyard.

But the second, inner section was the most special. From the outset the author makes note of the curtain that blocked the entrance to it. "Behind the second curtain was a second section called the Most Holy Place" (Hebrews **9:3**). This curtain blocked not only God's people from coming into God's presence, but even the priests. They could enter the Holy Place (the first section of the temple), but not the Most Holy Place. Only the high priest could enter, only once a year.

This inner chamber held the altar of incense and the ark of the covenant (**v 4**).

The ark was like a memory chest—a box full of things that are a treasure to you, that remind you of something. God put in this chest reminders of what he had done for his people: it was like a little history of Israel. God gave the Ten Commandments to get his covenant started. He made Aaron's staff blossom as a sign of his power and presence with his promised priests (Numbers 17:8). And he gave the people manna from heaven to preserve them in the wilderness. So the tablets, the staff, and the manna reminded them of what he had done.

> The ark was like a memory chest—it was like a little history of Israel.

But the real essence of the ark was the mercy seat. This was a picture of God's throne. It was where his presence dwelt (Leviticus 16:2). Around the mercy seat, on the lid of the ark, were the "cherubim of glory" (Hebrews **9:5**). These were angelic beings emblazoned in gold (see Exodus 25:20).

If, as the high priest, you had entered that inner chamber, you would have drawn back that curtain with a trembling hand, wondering whether you would come out alive (Leviticus 16:2-3). It would have been terrifying.

But as scary as it would have been, it was only ever a symbol of what God's real throne room is like in heaven. Remember Isaiah 6:1-5, where we find a vision of this true throne room. There are real angelic attendants flying around God's throne, covering their faces with their wings. The foundations shake and smoke fills the room when one of them speaks, yet even these wondrous, sinless angels are hiding their faces from God. And they sing, "Holy, holy, holy is the Lord of hosts; the whole earth is full of his glory!" (Isaiah 6:3)

What would you do if you walked into that real heavenly throne room? You certainly would not say, "Hey, God, I've been waiting to see you my whole life. I have some questions. Let's have a chat." No, you would say, like Isaiah, "Woe is me!" You would long for the ground to swallow you up. You would be utterly undone.

The ark of the covenant represented the presence of God, and in one sense, God was there. But this pales in comparison to what the ark was pointing toward. This is an example of the limitations of the old covenant. Even if you got into the temple—even if you got past that curtain—you still would not be in God's full presence. That is why the writer to the Hebrews wants his readers to know that they cannot rely on an earthly tent to solve their sin problem and get them into the presence of God.

But Jesus changed all that—as we'll see later in Hebrews 9.

## Earthly Priests

Hebrews **9:6-10** focuses on the earthly priests through whom the people worshiped. The normal priests spent a lot of time in the outer section "performing their ritual duties" (**v 6**)—that is, bringing in sacrifices, making sure the lamp didn't go out, making sure the bread was there. They did this "regularly." A better way to translate this Greek phrase, *dia pantos,* would be "repeatedly." That is, they were doing the same things again and again and again. They had to do this because the problem of sin was never solved. Later, in **verse 9**, we are told *why* these sacrifices didn't solve the problem of sin: "Gifts and sacrifices are offered that cannot perfect the conscience of the worshiper." It was all only *provisional*: "regulations for the body imposed until the time of reformation" (**v 10**). It pointed forward to the time of the new covenant—when the one person who could solve the problem of guilt would come.

In addition to describing the activity of the ordinary priests, our author tells us that "only the high priest" could go into the inner chamber, "and he but once a year, and not without taking blood" (**v 7**).

The high priest was the number one guy. He was the main representative of the people. He was the one who could enter the Most Holy Place. But this was still restricted. He could only come in once a year, to offer sacrifices for the people and for himself—and he had to do so very carefully.

Imagine that you are the high priest and you are about to pull back that curtain. You would be thinking, "How did my week go? How obedient have I been? How holy am I? Is this sacrifice going to be enough to clear my sin?" Even the high priest was an earthly person. He was still limited. So, he entered with trepidation.

All this tells us is that you cannot just stroll into God's presence in your current sinful state. You need someone to fix that problem.

Leviticus 16 is the chapter which gives the instructions for that yearly event when the high priest could enter the Most Holy Place. It was called the Day of Atonement. It is here that we see the problem most clearly. God says to Moses about Aaron, the first high priest, "Tell Aaron your brother not to come at any time into the Holy Place inside the veil, before the mercy seat that is on the ark, so that he may not die" (v 2).

Even Aaron, the brother of Moses, could not go in there without fear of death. The Day of Atonement was designed to allow him to enter in order to make offerings on behalf of the people of Israel; but he could only do so once he had gone through a series of rituals himself (Leviticus 16:3-14).

"By this," our author comments in Hebrews **9:8**, "the Holy Spirit indicates that the way into the holy places is not yet opened." If it was so difficult for an earthly priest to enter the earthly temple, how much more difficult would it be for an ordinary sinner to enter the true throne room of God? Under the old covenant, it was impossible.

The whole difference between the old covenant and the new covenant could be summarized in those two words, "not yet." Do you have full access to the holy God? In the Old Testament, the answer is "not yet." This could not happen "as long as the first section is still standing." In other words, as long as the old-covenant order—with its earthly tent—was still valid, then the way would be shut.

But the implication is that there was a time coming when God would open up the door fully and widely, and enable people to enter into his presence. The "present age" (**v 9**) of restriction would be over, and a new age of access would come.

It's worth looking back to Hebrews 4:16 at this point: "Let us then with confidence draw near to the throne of grace, that we may receive mercy and find grace to help in time of need." "Throne of grace" is equivalent in Greek to "mercy seat"—the seat on the ark of the covenant where God's presence rested.

What a contrast between the two covenants. Now, because of Jesus, you can enter God's presence *with confidence*. No more wondering if the sacrifice is enough. No more doubting whether you will be welcomed. In Christ, we know for sure we will be accepted.

## Fulfillment

The very first word in **9:11** is "But." *But* when Christ appeared, things changed. That is what the next section will tell us. All those limitations and barriers are gone. This is the glory of the new covenant.

"But when Christ appeared as a high priest" he entered "through the greater and more perfect tent"—the real throne room of heaven, not the earthly tent "of this creation." Like the high priest entering the Most Holy Place with the blood of animals, Jesus entered God's throne room "by means of his own blood" (**v 12**). He made a sacrifice for sin—and secured "an eternal redemption."

Notice the passage tells us that Jesus' journey into the holy places was "once for all." This stands in contrast to the never-ending work of the priests who kept repeating their activities over and over. Jesus' sacrifice was successful, so it only needed to be offered once.

The kind of cleansing that the old covenant provided was limited: it merely offered the "blood of goats and bulls," which only "sanctifies for the purification of the flesh" (**v 13**). This "purification" is what we might call ritual purity. The idea was that if you washed correctly, put on the right clothes, ate the right things, and performed the right rituals, you could be declared "clean." The book of Leviticus is full of these rituals. But all of this was just on the outside. Jesus, by contrast, has done something on the inside. He cleanses us internally. He sanctifies our hearts, not just our flesh. Thus, our author says, "How much more will the blood of Christ … purify our conscience" (**v 14**). It's an argument from the lesser to the greater. If a person thought the old-covenant sacrifices were beneficial, which only cleansed the outside, *how much more* would they think Christ's sacrifice is beneficial, which cleanses the inside!

There are a couple of reasons why Jesus' sacrifice was able to accomplish this cleansing. First, Jesus offered himself "through the eternal Spirit." The meaning of this phrase is debated and not altogether clear. But the word "eternal" has popped up many times before and often refers to Jesus' eternal nature as the divine Son of God. He is an effective high priest precisely because "he continues forever" (7:24). The only way to have an eternal sacrifice that is eternally sufficient is if one has an eternal Savior.

The second thing that makes his sacrifice unique was that he "offered himself without blemish." This is Old Testament language. Sacrificed animals had to be spotless, healthy, and strong. But Christ was "without blemish" in a more important sense: he was absolutely sinless. Thus, he alone is able to "purify our conscience from dead works to serve the living God" (**9:14**).

I am so thankful that we worship at a time when the work has been done. Jesus went not into the earthly tent but into the heavenly Most Holy Place. He was not just an earthly priest but the Son of God. And he offered not animals but himself. All of that solved the problem of limitations in the old covenant.

When I work in my office at the seminary, my staff knows that my research requires blocks of time when I can focus undisturbed. So, they are unlikely to just burst through my door and start talking to me unannounced. But that's not the case with my kids. When they come to visit me at the seminary, they just charge right into my office and jump up on my lap or give me a hug. Why do they feel able to be so bold? Because they are my children!

In the same way, we can now march boldly into the presence of God—not disrespectfully but with assurance that we will not be struck down—because God has poured out all his judgment on Christ in our place. Yes, God is still holy. But your sins have been paid for. And now you can run into your Father's arms like a little child. That is possible because of what Christ has done.

## Questions for reflection

1.  What features of the Old Testament tabernacle stood out to you and why?

2.  Does this passage change the way you think about the unprecedented access Christians have to God? What does more "confidence" look like (or not look like) as we come into God's presence?

3.  In what ways have you sought to alleviate a guilty conscience? How are you encouraged today to find that solution only at the cross?

# 8. NOTHING BUT THE BLOOD OF JESUS

"Why are Christians so obsessed with blood?"

So asked a non-Christian friend of mine. At first, I wasn't sure what he was talking about. But as I thought about it, I realized Christians really do talk about blood a lot. Just think about some well-known hymns: "Washed in the Blood," "Saved by the Blood of Jesus," "Nothing but the Blood of Jesus," and (perhaps most notably) "There Is a Fountain Filled with Blood."

Sometimes I think we don't pause enough to really think about the role of blood in our salvation. It means that someone's life had to be taken in our place. It means that our sin is a big deal—bigger than we think—and demands a terrible price.

In the next section of Hebrews 9, as the author continues his comparison between the old covenant and the new, we have an opportunity to pause and think. It shows us both the seriousness of sin and, at the same time, the depth of God's love. It shows why Christ's sacrifice was necessary and what it achieved.

## An Eternal Inheritance

"[Jesus] is the mediator of a new covenant so that those who are called may receive the promised eternal inheritance" (**v 15**). The author uses that language of inheritance very deliberately because he is going to make an **analogy** about a will. You can't see it in the English translations, but "will" and "covenant" are the same word in Greek. That is why our author says, "A will is involved" (**v 16**).

Jesus has a great inheritance stored up for you, but you can't receive it unless he—the person who made the will—passes away. "A will takes effect only at death" (**v 17**). Death is the pathway to inheritance. We "receive the promised eternal inheritance" because "a death has occurred" (**v 15**).

At its core, this inheritance won by Jesus involves the forgiveness of sins. The "transgressions committed under the first covenant" could never be cleansed by the sacrifices of animals, but they could be cleansed by Jesus' death.

No doubt this "inheritance" implies other benefits that flow naturally from our forgiveness. That would include our future resurrection—being raised from the dead and given a new resurrected body. And with that body we will enjoy the new heavens and new earth. But the greatest part of the inheritance is Jesus himself. He is the great reward. What we are most looking forward to is being with Jesus eternally.

## The Need for Blood

Of course, Jesus' death was not the first time blood was shed. As our author reminds us, "Therefore not even the first covenant was inaugurated without blood" (**v 18**). In other words, things have always been this way. God has always been holy. Sin has always been a big deal. Someone has always had to pay.

In Moses' time, when the people first agreed to the covenant, he sprinkled blood on them (**v 19-20**; see Exodus 24:7-8). Water, scarlet wool, and branches of hyssop (Hebrews **9:19**) were also part of the purification rituals (Numbers 19:1-6).

But blood is the main symbol. "Under the law almost everything is purified with blood" (Hebrews **9:22**). Blood would be sprinkled over the altar, inside the tabernacle, and even inside the Most Holy

Place where the ark of the covenant was (**v 21**; e.g. Leviticus 4:4-7; 16:14-16).

We often don't realize what a gruesome scene this would have been: blood on the floor, blood on the altar, blood on the hands of the priest and on his garments, blood on the people. But it sent a clear theological message: the effect of sin is very serious.

In Hebrews **9:20**, our author cites Exodus 24:8, the words used by Moses to inaugurate the old covenant: "This is the blood of the covenant." Nearly the same wording was used by Jesus when he inaugurated the new covenant at the Lord's Supper: "This is *my* blood of the covenant" (Matthew 26:28).

When we remember the cross by sharing the Lord's Supper, we should be hearing the same message that Old Testament Israelites heard when they went to make sacrifices at the temple. In order to participate in a covenant with God—in order to be purified and forgiven and to gain access to him—you need blood.

Yet in the new covenant there is a difference: the blood that is shed is *Jesus'* blood, the only blood which can take away sin. Jesus made an important change to what Moses said: "*my* blood." He loved you so much that he gave himself for you.

This fundamental need for Christ's blood is summed up in Hebrews **9:22**: "Without the shedding of blood there is no forgiveness of sins."

There are two fundamental principles of theology behind that verse.

The first principle is that our sin is a bigger deal than we tend to think it is. It is a cosmic rebellion against the rightful King of the universe, which deserves the penalty of death.

This was true right from the start. In the Garden of Eden, God told Adam and Eve that if they ate the fruit of the tree of the knowledge of good and evil, they would surely die (Genesis 2:17). Death is and has always been the punishment for sin.

The second principle is that God is holier than we tend to think he is. We often imagine God as just a bigger version of ourselves, and so we come to think of him as the problem. Why can't he just put up with our sin? But here is the reality: God is pure, holy righteousness. God is so holy that he cannot dwell with sin; and he is so concerned with justice that he cannot simply forget about sin.

There is not a single sin committed in all of time that God will allow to go unpunished. Either God punishes that sin in us, or he punishes it in our substitute, Christ. Sin is a monumental problem requiring a monumental solution. That is why Christ had to come.

When we diminish either the seriousness of sin or the holiness of God in order to make people feel better, we end up diminishing what Christ has done for us. If sin were not a big deal or God were not holy, then we would not really need Jesus to have died on the cross, and the gospel would no longer be gloriously good news.

This is why the old covenant involved so much blood. It made people realize how serious the problem of sin was.

## Jesus Appeared in the Presence of God

The purification rites under the old covenant were important, but at the same time the author reminds us again that the temple and its altar were just "copies of the heavenly things" (Hebrews **9:23**). So, the purification could only be symbolic.

Jesus, however, "entered, not into holy places made with hands, which are copies of the true things, but into heaven itself, now to appear in the presence of God on our behalf" (**v 24**).

One of the most poignant (and frightening) pictures of God's heavenly throne room is in Revelation 4. There we see that the symbols of the earthly tabernacle have a true, heavenly counterpart. The earthly tabernacle had a "door" or curtain, and so the heavenly one has a door, and it stands open (v 1). The earthly ark of the covenant was understood to be symbolic of God's throne, but in Revelation we have the real throne (v 2). On top of the earthly ark were golden angelic creatures (cherubim), but in Revelation they are real and surround the throne (v 8). In this heavenly tabernacle we even have a sevenfold golden lampstand, but this one shines with the very power of God's Spirit (v 5).

So, Christ did what no human being had ever done—he went into this throne room, representing his people before God's holy presence.

No matter what kind of life you have led and no matter what sins you struggle with currently, if you are trusting in Christ, then, when God looks upon you, he sees perfect righteousness because of the blood shed for you by Jesus. If you are a Christian, then God will not reject you. To do so he would also be rejecting his own Son. And that is not going to happen.

So this is our great hope: the hope of representation. You cannot represent yourself before God. But Jesus represents you perfectly.

He is your advocate, your spokesman, and your intercessor. He represents us both in his death and in his life. He has died in our place; it is as if we have died and paid the penalty for our sin (Romans 6:6). He has lived the perfect life of righteousness; it is as if we have lived perfectly (1 Corinthians 1:30; 2 Corinthians 5:21). Jesus is, in effect, saying to God, *What is true of me is true of all those who put their faith and trust in me.*

That means we can be honest about who we are. If you know God is never going to reject you, then you do not need to be afraid of anyone discovering what you are really like. God accepts you solely on the work that Christ has done.

## Jesus Offered Himself

Anyone who entered into the real Most Holy Place instead of its earthly copy would need to offer "better sacrifices" (**9:23**). And that is what Christ did.

**Verse 25** is critical. The high priest enters the Most Holy Place every year "with blood not his own." But Jesus, by contrast, went only once, with his own blood.

The high priest had to keep repeating this act of sacrifice again and again because he brought the blood of an animal, which could not achieve real **remission of sins**. But Christ did not have to keep making his offering. His blood was superior: the perfect sacrifice for sin. So, "he has appeared once for all at the end of the ages to put away sin by the sacrifice of himself" (**v 26**).

The phrase "end of the ages" is significant because it echoes the very beginning of the book where the author has told us that the coming of Jesus has inaugurated "the last days" (1:2). It tells us that the coming of Jesus is the culmination and pinnacle of all God's promises: the crescendo of all God's redemptive plan. There's nothing greater or better.

The implication of that fact is hard to miss. If Christ has ushered in a new age—the climax of history—then why go back to the old ways? Why would a person want to go back to the old covenant when we now have what is new and more wonderful?

All this means that we can be confident that there is nothing more to do to solve the problem of sin.

In our earthly lives, there is always something more to do. Whether you've got to get the laundry done or mow the lawn or take the kids to school or cook dinner, there is always something. And that is just on an earthly level. But what about in eternity? What if you had the stress of continually having to work to earn your salvation? What if you feared that that work would never be finished—not ever?

> We need someone who can bear the brunt of the storm.

Jesus changes the game. He offered himself once. Our author says it in **9:26** and then again in **verse 28**: "having been offered once to bear the sins of many." He will not let this idea go because it is so important. Indeed, it is the heart of the gospel. The good news is not that there's something that *can* be done, but that something has *already* been done. It is finished.

That matters for us because we too will die and face judgment. In **verse 27** the author draws an analogy between our death and Christ's death. "Just as it is appointed for man to die once, and after that comes judgment, so Christ..."

There are two inescapable, sobering facts here. One is that you're going to die someday. The second is that when you die, you'll face judgment. It is inevitable.

I can still remember when Hurricane Dorian was rumbling through the Atlantic in 2019, headed ominously toward the east coast of the United States. Since we live in North Carolina, we pay attention to approaching hurricanes. Dorian was the one of the strongest Atlantic hurricanes in recorded history, a Category 5 with winds reaching 185 mph. So powerful was it that the "rumblings" could be picked up by seismometers while it was still far out in the Atlantic.

God's judgment is like a hurricane heading toward your town. It's not here yet, but we can see it on the horizon. We can feel the rumblings. It is an enormous, terrifying inevitability heading our way. We can't avoid it. We can't run from it. We cannot wish it away. In such a scenario, we need a place of refuge. We need someone who can bear the brunt of the storm for us. The good news is that Christ has been "offered once to bear the sins of many" (**v 28**). He died once and faced judgment once, on behalf of every single person who trusts in him. Only he can do this. Only he can save us from the judgment to come.

## Jesus Will Return

Christ came from heaven to earth to die for our sins, once for all. Then he went back to heaven to represent us before God. Our third hope is that he is going to return again to bring us home.

This is all in **verse 28**. He "will appear a second time, not to deal with sin but to save those who are eagerly waiting for him."

When my kids were younger, whenever I was coming back from a trip, I would pull into the driveway and see them all waiting for me on the front step. They knew my flight had landed, and they were eagerly waiting for me to come back. Those days are long gone now! But I remember seeing their eyes light up as they saw me: "Dad's home." They were waiting eagerly.

That is not always the way we feel when we think about Christ's return. Of course, in the abstract we are looking forward to Christ coming back, but we are not always really all that eager about it. So what would it look like to eagerly wait for the return of Jesus? First, we need to make sure we don't grow too comfortable in this world. The more we make this place our home, the less we will long for our heavenly home. We must always remember that we are strangers and aliens here so that we look forward to the time when we can return to our true homeland.

Second, we need to continually cast off the works of darkness, re-placing them with the works of righteousness. If we are caught up in sin patterns we won't relinquish, then we will not be eager for Christ to return anytime soon. In short, we need to be ready for his return. As in the parable of the ten virgins, we need to have our lamps burn-ing brightly when he comes back (Matthew 25:1-13).

Third, we need to regularly stir our affections for Jesus. We will only long for his coming if we long for him. Think of a wife whose husband is away on a long journey. In anticipation of his return, she looks at his picture and reads his letters, reminding herself of why she loves him. So it is with Jesus. We read his word and fellowship with him in prayer, so that we are more eager to be with him again.

In sum, we need to be sitting on that front step saying, "I cannot wait until my Lord returns to save me and bring me home." We may not know when it will come; but because of what Christ has already done, we can look forward to that day with certainty. Jesus has already dealt with sin; he is coming back to bring us to himself at last.

# Questions for reflection

1. What aspects of your "inheritance" in Christ are you most looking forward to? How are some of those blessings present in your life already?

2. In what ways might you have underplayed the seriousness of your sin, or the seriousness of God's holiness?

3. How would looking forward to the second coming affect your life in the present?

## PART TWO

Some of my favorite movies are those that have a twist at the end—something I never saw coming. As soon as I recover from the initial shock, there's always something I want to do immediately: watch the movie *again*. Why? Because I want to see the clues and indications that I missed. It is only after I know the ending that I can go back and identify them for what they are.

The Bible kind of works that way. Having seen the remarkable way God brings redemption through Jesus, we can go back and read the Old Testament again with fresh eyes. And we will see things that we never saw before. We can see how things were always pointing to Jesus, even when we didn't catch them the first time.

In Hebrews **10:1-18** our author takes a similar approach. He has spent a lot of time showing the limitations of the old-covenant system of worship. But now he is going to argue that this message is really nothing new. The idea that animal sacrifices are provisional and that God is not fully pleased by them is not found just in the New Testament; it is found in the Old Testament too! Abandoning those sacrifices and turning to Jesus was God's plan for us from the start.

In short, the author wants us to go back and read the Old Testament afresh. When we do, we will see clues about the limitations of animal sacrifices everywhere.

This would have been a very powerful argument for the recipients of this letter. Remember, they were largely Jewish Christians who were thinking about returning to the old sacrificial system. But the writer wants to show them that, if they look back through the Old Testament, they will see that God's plan for a new and better system was always there. Doing away with the old sacrificial system was not a left turn out of the blue. The Jews could—maybe even should—have seen it coming.

## Reasons Not to Go Back

The old covenant was not false or wrong. But it was provisional and partial. "The law has but a shadow of the good things to come instead of the true form of these realities" (**v 1**).

For a while when my wife and I were dating, I was in California and she was in North Carolina. That's nearly 3,000 miles apart. There was no internet back then, so we wrote letters to one another. These days, when people date long distance, they keep in touch via video calls. They can at least see the person they are dating. That is much better than letters; but it is still not as good as being together in person—when you can hold hands and talk face to face.

The difference between an online relationship and an in-person relationship is kind of like the difference between the old covenant and the new covenant. One does not contradict the other. But one is clearly "better" than the other!

This is what our author means when he calls the old covenant order a "shadow of the good things to come." A shadow is not contradictory to the person that makes it; and it can provide a vague, general outline of what that person is like. But no one prefers the shadow if they can have the real thing.

Because these sacrifices were only shadows—only provisional—they could "never ... make perfect those who draw near."

Our author appeals to basic logic to prove that this is true. If the old-covenant sacrifices had worked, "would they not have ceased to be offered?" (**v 2**). In other words, the repetitive nature of animal sacrifices should have been a clue that they could not be the final thing you trust in.

Moreover, if the old-covenant sacrifices had been effective, then the worshiper "would no longer have [had] any consciousness of sins." This is not a reference merely to a person's *awareness* of their own sinfulness—that is something that we continue to experience even after trusting Christ. No, it refers to an assurance that the worshiper no longer stands guilty under the wrath of God (see verse 22).

That is what the old sacrificial system, in and of itself, could never provide.

At this point, one might wonder why the old-covenant order was instituted at all. What was it really accomplishing? One thing is that these sacrifices were "a reminder of sin every year" (**v 3**). In that sense, they were not a waste of time. They may not have been able to save you from your sins, but they did remind you of your need for a Savior.

> Jesus offered himself out of love. It was personal.

The truth is that the old-covenant system was gospel-oriented. Nowhere did anyone say, *You're fine as you are and if you work hard enough, you can get to heaven.* No, the message of the sacrifices was repeatedly, *You're not okay. You are a sinner. Blood needs to be shed on your behalf.*

The purity laws in Leviticus also reveal this. If you touched a corpse, if you didn't wash in a certain way, if you didn't avoid certain foods, then you were unclean. The message couldn't be missed; you always needed cleansing.

But the blood of animals couldn't provide that cleansing. "It is impossible for the blood of bulls and goats to take away sins" (**v 4**).

Impossible. No matter how many bulls or goats you offer, how impressive they are, or how frequently you offer them, the blood of animals cannot take away sin.

So, the sacrificial system also shows you that no effort you make, no matter how well-intended, could ever be enough to save you from your sins.

But there is glorious good news. God promised he would send a sacrifice that does save. Our author now gives us three reasons to trust in the sacrifice of Christ for us.

## Christ Offers His Body

The first reason we can trust in Christ is because he offered his own body—a physical human body—as a sacrifice for us (**v 5**). To prove his point, the author invites his audience to look back at Psalm 40 and see that God always said that this would happen. This would have been a powerful argument for the original Jewish Christian audience who took the Old Testament seriously.

It is noteworthy that our author cites Psalm 40:6-8 as the words of Jesus. "When Christ came into the world, he said…" How can that be so, since David was the writer of Psalm 40? Because he wrote it under the influence of the Holy Spirit. With hindsight, we can see that these words are about Jesus—and it was actually Jesus speaking through David's mouth.

The citation of Psalm 40 begins with the speaker (who we now know is Jesus) observing that the normal sacrificial system is not enough: "Sacrifices and offerings you have not desired" (Hebrews **10:5**). He repeats the idea again in **verse 6**: "In burnt offerings and sin offerings you have taken no pleasure." We see here that the Old Testament itself acknowledged the limitations in the sacrificial system.

But then the speaker in Psalm 40 declares that God has something better than these sacrifices: "A body have you prepared for me" (Hebrews **10:5**). This is an anticipation of the **incarnation**. Christ's priesthood would not be about offering animal sacrifices but about offering his own body.

"Behold, I have come to do your will, O God," continues Jesus (**v 7**). His job was to do what the Father told him to do. He willingly, consciously, and intentionally gave his body for his people. This is another contrast with animal sacrifices. A lamb does not wake up in the morning and think to itself, "I'd like to die for sinners today." Christ, unlike a lamb, did not die because he was forced into it; he went forward *willingly*.

That is the picture of love. He was not just given for you; he gave himself for you. The sacrificial system was impersonal, distant, external—it was easy for it to become just a matter of performing the rites. But Jesus offered himself out of love. It was personal.

**Verses 8-9** provide a sort of commentary on Psalm 40. In Hebrews **10:8**, our author refers again to **verses 5-6**, to say that God has "neither desired nor taken pleasure in sacrifices and offerings." He further clarifies that this portion of Psalm 40 is referring to the ordinary animal sacrifices "offered according to the law."

Moreover, in Hebrews **10:9** our author affirms that these old sacrifices have been superseded by what Christ has done by giving his body. Christ "abolishes the first in order to establish the second." In other words, our author interprets Psalm 40 as Jesus doing away with the old system of animal sacrifices in favor of establishing a new system focused on the one-time giving of his body.

To be clear, when Psalm 40 says that God did not delight in the old-covenant sacrifices, this is not to suggest that the old covenant was in error, or that these sacrifices were offered contrary to his will. It simply means that these sacrifices were not satisfactory to him as a way to really take away sins. Something more would be needed.

The gift of Jesus' body leads to a wonderful result: "We have been sanctified" (Hebrews **10:10**). The word "sanctified" here is in the perfect tense in Greek. This speaks to a completed action with ongoing implications or effects in the present. Thus, this verse is unlikely to refer to *progressive* sanctification—in which we become more Christ-like over time by the power of the Spirit. Rather, it probably refers to *positional* sanctification: namely, that we have been cleansed by Christ and set apart, once for all, for his service. We are in a new position, having moved from the realm of darkness into the realm of the light.

## Christ Sat Down

**Verses 11-14** add a second reason to trust in Christ's sacrifice. We know that it was successful because he sat down.

Here is the logic. There was no chair in the tabernacle. The priests would never rest because their work was never done. They kept standing, "offering repeatedly" ineffectual sacrifices (**v 11**).

But Christ offered a single sacrifice and then "sat down at the right hand of God" (**v 12**). Unlike the priest, Jesus has finished his work and has sat down. (We previously saw this in Hebrews 1:3, and it was also hinted at in 8:1.)

In **10:13** we are told what Jesus does next from that position at the right hand of God. He is waiting "until his enemies should be made a footstool for his feet." For Jesus to sit at the right hand of the Father means that someday all his enemies will be destroyed.

This is an allusion to Psalm 110:1, the same psalm that mentioned Melchizedek. Our author has also quoted and alluded to this particular verse before, in Hebrews 1:13 and 2:8. "The Lord said to my Lord, 'Sit at my right hand until I make your enemies a footstool.'" Essentially, the point is that Jesus is in a position of power. Sitting at the right hand of God means that he rules the world and will judge the world. "Everything [is] in subjection to him" (2:8).

Although the picture of Jesus as a sacrificial lamb may tempt us to think of him as meek and mild, we must not forget that he is also a lion who will tear his enemies to pieces. He will reign supreme and defeat all his foes. Jesus is the lion *and* the lamb. He is multidimensional.

It is not just that Jesus' enemies will be defeated. Think about that footstool image. Jesus will put his feet over the top of his enemies and squash them down. They will be totally subjected to him. Satan himself will be crushed by Jesus' feet (Genesis 3:15; Romans 16:20).

Like the prior section (Hebrews **10:5-10**), the final verse of this section also ends with a statement about the benefits of Christ's work: "He has perfected for all time those who are being sanctified" (**v 14**). The idea of "perfection" has dominated these last few chapters (7:11; 7:19; 9:9; **10:1**), but each time it has been mentioned to show what the old sacrificial system was *unable* to do. The law could not really cleanse our sins and make us presentable to the holy God.

Now, however, it is used *positively*. What the old covenant could not accomplish in many offerings, Christ accomplished "by a single offering" (**v 14**). Even more than that, this perfection won't ever end—it is "for all time."

The term "sanctified" also pops up again here in **verse 14**, but this time our author uses the present participle ("*being* sanctified"). It's possible, therefore, that he has progressive sanctification in mind, referring to the ongoing work of the Spirit in making us holier over time. On the other hand, we may not want to press the present tense too hard given that other passages use sanctification language in a more positional sense (**10:10**; 10:29; 13:12). Regardless, this sanctification is still rooted in the cleansing work of Christ, which makes us "perfect." Because we are truly forgiven, we are now empowered to live more and more for Christ.

## The Spirit Assures Us

The third and final reason to trust in Christ's sacrifice is found in **10:15-18**, where the author quotes again from Jeremiah 31.

He introduces this quotation by saying that "the Holy Spirit also bears witness to us" (Hebrews **10:15**). Our author sees the words of Jeremiah as the words of the Holy Spirit—the words of God. This is another wonderful example of how our author demonstrates the way we should approach the Old Testament. It is authoritative because it has been **inspired** by the Holy Spirit. And it is all about Jesus.

How do these words of the Spirit help us trust in the new-covenant sacrifice of Christ? First, we are reminded that God promised this new covenant long ago (**v 16**). The idea that the old covenant would pass away, and that a new sacrificial system would come, was always part of God's plan.

And this time things would be different. With a special outpouring of the Holy Spirit, this new message of redemption would be received and internalized: "I will put my laws on their hearts, and write them on their minds."

Second, God promises that this time the cleansing of sin will *really* happen. The sacrifice will be fully effectual. Thus, God can say, "I will remember their sins and their lawless deeds no more" (**v 17**).

With these truths in mind, our author is able to make a final declaration about the old covenant system. He can now declare, "there is no longer any offering for sin" (**v 18**). What he means is that we no longer need animal sacrifices according to the old-covenant order. Why? Because "there is forgiveness" in what Christ has done.

What a beautiful truth on which to end this section. All of redemptive history, all of the work of Christ, all of the plans of the Father, have been aimed at this solitary goal: *that sins might be forgiven.*

Our world needs that message now. Indeed, our churches need that message now. It seems that people want to make Christianity first and foremost about all sorts of other things: being a good person, helping others, fighting for social change, and so on. But we can't forget the core message. Christianity is a message about sin and how we can be forgiven for it.

Paul would agree: "The saying is trustworthy and deserving of full acceptance, that Christ Jesus came into the world to save sinners, of whom I am the foremost" (1 Timothy 1:15).

## Questions for reflection

1. How does this passage better help you understand the relationship between the Old Testament and the New?

2. How might this passage change the way you view the Lord's Supper?

3. How does this passage show Jesus as both lion and lamb? Do you think you have a balanced view of Jesus as both of those things?

# 9. DON'T QUIT

Do you ever wonder what the theme of the whole Bible is? What's the single concept that holds it all together? There are many possible answers to that question. But arguably, Jeremiah 31:33 captures it pretty well: "And I will be their God, and they shall be my people." In fact, our author already cited this passage earlier in the book (Hebrews 8:10).

But that is not the only place in which it occurs. In fact, this concept—in one form or another—recurs throughout the whole Bible (Genesis 17:8; Exodus 29:45; Ezekiel 14:11; Zechariah 8:8; 2 Corinthians 6:16). Indeed, this is the crescendo at the end of the book of Revelation: "Behold, the dwelling place of God is with man. He will dwell with them, and they will be his people, and God himself will be with them as their God" (21:3).

In short, God desires to be with us. That's the big point of the Bible.

At the same time, we need to acknowledge that being near God is a scary place to be. Whenever people come into God's presence, it can be crushing. Remember the story of Isaiah 6: even a holy prophet like Isaiah declares, "Woe is me!" when he encounters the living God.

So, drawing near to God is a complex affair.

But with Christ's perfect sacrifice paving the way, drawing near is not just a possibility; it's what we are called to do! So, in the next section, Hebrews **10:19-22**, our author reminds us again of the wonderful privilege of drawing near to God. Then the rest of the chapter encourages us to live in a way that is worthy of the God who has been so gracious to us—we are to persevere and not to fall away.

## Draw Near!

In a few verses (**v 19-22**), our author summarizes all the themes in the prior chapters about Jesus and what he has done for us.

"We have confidence to enter the holy places by the blood of Jesus" (**v 19**). By now we should be clear that "the holy place" doesn't mean the earthly temple but heaven itself. We can now enter God's presence with confidence.

Jesus' blood has opened the way "through the curtain, that is, through his flesh" (**v 20**). This imagery comes from the tabernacle. Remember that big curtain that blocked off the inner section of the temple? When Christ's flesh was torn for you, the temple curtain was also torn—literally torn in two (Matthew 27:51). It was a physical sign of a spiritual reality. Now you can "walk" straight into the Most Holy Place.

What does this do for us as believers? It doesn't mean that we draw near to God physically but that we draw near to him spiritually. We can come into his holy presence without fear and doubt. Now, through Christ's blood, we can approach God's throne in prayer with confidence that he loves us and hears us. It means that we can confess our sins to God, not out of fear of judgment but in hope of forgiveness.

This pathway to God is a "new and living way." It is "new" because Jesus has inaugurated a new covenant. It is "living" because we do not have a dead Savior. Sacrificed animals would stay dead, but Jesus came to life again at the resurrection. Now he lives to intercede for us; he is eternally there for us. He is "a great priest over the house of God" (Hebrews **10:21**).

If you said in the Old Testament context that someone was a priest over the house of God, you would mean over the physical temple or tabernacle. But now the term is used to refer to God's people. Wherever God's people are, that is where God's house is—and Christ is over that house.

When Jesus spoke with the **Samaritan** woman at the well, she brought up the disagreement between Jews and Samaritans about where people should worship (John 4:20). But Jesus answered, "The hour is coming when neither on this mountain nor in Jerusalem will you worship the Father ... The hour is coming, and is now here, when the true worshipers will worship the Father in spirit and in truth" (v 21, 23).

Geography and physical buildings no longer matter: under the new covenant you can worship God wherever you are. That means that everybody all over the globe can draw near to God through what Christ has done.

That is the culmination of Hebrews **10:19-22**. Since we have this better sacrifice, and since we have this better priest, "let us draw near" (**v 22**).

We do not need to have the fear and trepidation that an old covenant believer would have had—uncertain of whether they really wanted to draw near to this holy God. No, we have "confidence" (**v 19**) and "full assurance" (**v 22**).

This confidence does not mean saying, "God is lucky to have me on his team." Our confidence is about who Christ is and what he has done. So, our approach to God is humble: we recognize that we do not deserve what we have been given. We can walk into God's presence with assurance that he loves us; yet this is not because we are great but only because in Christ he has redeemed us.

At the same time, we can also have assurance about the state of our own hearts. We can draw near "with a true heart" (**v 22**). Why? Because "our hearts [have been] sprinkled clean from an evil conscience and our bodies washed with pure water."

Under the old covenant, as we read in 9:19-22, the priests would sprinkle the blood of animals over objects in the temple to purify them. Likewise, Christ's blood—figuratively speaking—has been sprinkled on your heart, renewing it so that you have new life.

Similarly, under the old covenant, if you became ritually unclean for any reason, you would have to wash. All these washes pointed to the real cleansing that Christ would bring. Our author is not saying that you have literally had a bath; he is saying that you are clean in the eyes of God. You've not just been washed with earthly water; you've been washed with "pure water" (**10:22**), the kind that only Christ can offer.

The promise of Jeremiah 31, which our author quoted in Hebrews 8:8-12 and 10:16-17, has been fulfilled. We have a new covenant, a clean conscience, and a new heart. That is why we can draw near to God in confidence and assurance.

## How to Hold Fast

One of the heroes of J.R.R. Tolkien's *The Lord of the Rings* is a hobbit named Frodo Baggins, whose quest throughout the trilogy is to travel to Mordor and destroy the evil Ring of Power in the fires of Mount Doom. But Frodo is accompanied by his loyal friend Samwise Gamgee, who walks alongside him, encourages him, and reminds him of the truth—that their journey is the only hope for their world. There is no way Frodo would ever have made it to Mordor without Sam, who even carries his friend up the mountain at the very end.

> You can't do faith alone. You need someone to stoke the fire.

Tolkien's work is a vision of the Christian life. If we are to remain faithful in the long and difficult journey of the Christian life, Sam is an example of what is needed. Sam embodies two principles that are key. First, he holds fast to his beliefs about their mission without wavering; and second, he walks together with Frodo as a friend and encourager.

In other words, he provides both *truth* and *community*. These are the two principles that our author presents in **verses 23-25**, which will keep you from falling away and bring you to your destination.

First, our author addresses the issue of truth: "Let us hold fast the confession of our hope without wavering, for he who promised is faithful" (**v 23**).

"Confession" refers to the content of what we believe. We must not waver from what we know is true.

Sometimes people have a negative perception of theology or doctrine. Perhaps they are tired of hearing about disagreements between theologians or **denominations**, and they decide that it is better not to talk about theology at all. Or perhaps they have listened to the world's message: that what matters is not truth but your own subjective experience—that you can feel your own way to God, and that is more important than knowing the truth about him.

But if you are going to stay the course, you need to know what you believe and why.

In our modern day we are bombarded with every reason to give up on what we believe. People think Christianity is ridiculous or offensive or crazy. People attack core Christian truths on the internet and in books. We need to be careful to hold on because we are under great temptation to drift away.

Of course, we do sometimes doubt the truth of what we believe. But I think that's why our author adds this little phrase at the end of **verse 23**: "for he who promised is faithful." Remember, God is trustworthy in what he's promised. His word will prove true in the end. That is the motivation for our perseverance.

The second thing you need is not doctrinal but relational: "Let us consider how to stir up one another to love and good works, not neglecting to meet together, as is the habit of some, but encouraging one another" (**v 24-25**). Faith is one of those things you can't do alone. Many people try to. Perhaps they have had bad experiences in church or perhaps they just don't see why they should make the commitment. But we need each other. We need to "stir up one another to love and good works."

You need someone to stoke the fire in you, to keep you on the right track, to help you get up when you don't want to, and to shake you occasionally and tell you to get it together. You need to be part of a team—with teammates who will help, encourage, push, rebuke, and love you, and whom you can help, encourage, push, rebuke, and love.

Are you a committed member of a Bible-believing, Christ-loving church? If not, you are going to have to face all the challenges of life by yourself—with no one there to lift and stir you up. You will find it hard to keep going in the Christian faith.

This is the theme picked up in the next passage.


## Don't Fall Away

**Verses 26-31** are another warning against apostasy. Don't fall away! Specifically, do not be those who "go on sinning deliberately" (**v 26**).

The words "go on" and "deliberately" are important here. Even true believers fall into sin sometimes. But an apostate is someone who knows how serious sin is—who has "received knowledge of the truth" (**v 26**)—but goes on sinning, repeatedly and deliberately.

It is people who *repent* of their sin who have a right relationship with Jesus. Think of the story Jesus tells about the **Pharisee** and the tax collector who both pray in the temple (Luke 18:9-14). The Pharisee boasts to God about what a good person he is. But the tax collector says, "God, be merciful to me, a sinner!" And Jesus comments that it is the tax collector who goes away justified.

If you know about the grace of God in Christ, yet sin unrepentantly and chronically, you are actively rejecting Christ. This is expressed in Hebrews **10:29**: the person who does this "has trampled underfoot the Son of God, and has profaned the blood of the covenant by which he was sanctified, and has outraged the Spirit of grace."

"Mock," "show disdain," or "insult" would also be good renderings of the word translated as "trampled underfoot." That is what you are doing to Jesus when you stubbornly and willfully embrace sin.

When someone in the church turns their back on their faith, they are also rejecting all the gifts they have been given as part of the **visible church**.

They have received the knowledge of the truth (**v 26**). Perhaps they have professed belief in Christ without ever really directing their hearts toward him. It is important to realize that mere intellectual assent to truths is not what is meant by being a Christian.

They have also lived God's way, at least in an external sense. They were "sanctified" (**v 29**). It's clear from the context that "sanctified" here is not a genuine heart change but an outward conformity. This person lives the right way. But even this doesn't make someone a true follower of Christ. You don't have to believe in Christ to live in a moral way.

Think about all the blessings and privileges a person has enjoyed who has been part of the church and professed to be a Christian! They have the truth of God's word preached to them; they have the fellowship of Christians; they enjoy the presence of the Holy Spirit in that community, even if not in them personally. And yet in the end some still reject Christ.

## A Terrible Path

Our passage offers a frightening description of anyone who turns their back on Christ. They are among God's "adversaries"—that is, his enemies—and this means that they are awaiting "a fury of fire" (**v 27**).

Our author is probably alluding to Old Testament examples of judgment. God rained down fire on the sinful cities of Sodom and Gomorrah (Genesis 19:24), and consumed Nadab and Abihu with fire when they made false offerings (Leviticus 10:1-2). You may hear stories like that and wish they weren't in the Bible. But they show us who God really is. God is holy and just as well as loving. He sent Jesus to save us; but if we reject Jesus, we are left only with judgment.

We have learned in the previous chapters of Hebrews that Jesus is the only way into the true throne room of God—the only way we can safely stand before the holy God. If you reject him, what other path do you have to get to God? There is none. So "there no longer remains a sacrifice for sins" (Hebrews **10:26**).

If you reject Jesus by embracing sin, then when you stand before the holy God, there will be no intercession and no mediator—just your sins, laid out bare. That is why all the apostate is left with is "a fearful expectation of judgment" (**v 27**).

But our author takes things one step further. It's not that the apostate will just receive judgment—all unbelievers will receive that. No, apostates will receive "worse punishment" (**v 29**). Why? Because they have received immense and unprecedented privileges and still, after all of that, they have spurned Christ.

To make this point, our author draws a comparison with the situation under the old covenant. Sure, people "who ... set aside the law of Moses" were subject to judgment (**v 28**). But if God punished people for sin under the law, "how much more" (**v 29**) will he punish those who reject his Son even after fully understanding the truth of his grace? If people were punished for rejecting Moses, then how much more for rejecting Jesus! After all, God is the one "who said, 'Vengeance is mine; I will repay.' And again, 'The Lord will judge his people'" (**v 30**). These two quotations are from Deuteronomy 32:35-36. God has always been a God who judges sin. He repays those who reject him.

That is why the passage concludes, "It is a fearful thing to fall into the hands of the living God" (Hebrews **10:31**).

This is a Bible verse worth memorizing. It is theological ballast which will prevent your ship from listing. When people try to tell you that God doesn't do judgment, this verse will remind you that he is a holy God who cares about sin.

And he is "the living God"—not an idol, not made of wood and stone. He is alive, and you can have a relationship with him through Christ. But without Christ, what are you left with?

That is the somber warning of this passage. Do not turn your back on all the great things God has done for you already. If you do, the only thing left for you is judgment.

# Questions for reflection

1.  How are you doing today with your confidence and assurance about drawing near to our holy God? How has this passage helped you?

2.  How important have doctrine and theology been in your life? Are there areas in which you feel that you are wavering about what you believe? How does this passage help?

3.  How does this passage help you to know how to better help people caught by sin?

## PART TWO

### The Antidote to Apostasy

Not long ago I was watching a fascinating documentary on the selection process for Navy SEALs. These are the members of the most elite military organization in the US—the specialists of the specialists of the specialists. Part of the initial training is known as "hell week." The job of the trainers in that week is to weed people out.

They put the recruits through day after day of every rigorous exercise you can possibly imagine: lifting huge poles on their shoulder, running crazy distances, paddling boats out on the ocean. The soldiers are wet, they are cold, and they are not allowed to sleep for more than a few hours. Sometimes they are not even allowed to eat. By day two they are wiped; by day three they cannot see straight; by day four they are falling asleep where they stand.

If you want to quit, all you have to do is to ring a bell in the center of the camp. All the time, the trainers are screaming at you that you should go and ring the bell. Then you can go home and have a hot shower, and it will all be over. "Just ring the bell." That is the voice continually in the recruits' ears.

But what fascinated me in this documentary was that there was another voice. As soon as the other soldiers saw someone get up and go toward the bell, they would say to him, "No, don't quit! Don't do it!"

There were two reasons these soldiers would give for not quitting. The first was "Look how far you've come." *If you quit now, everything you've endured so far was a waste. Look how much you have accomplished, and don't throw it all away.* The second reason was "Think about your goal." *If you can get through this, you get to put on that uniform and become a Navy SEAL.*

Hebrews **10:32-39** has the same strategy. It provides two motivations for not quitting the Christian life. First, *look how far you've come.* Second, *think about how much you will gain if you make it to the end.*

In short, to persevere we need to learn *look back* and also to *look forward*. Together, these constitute the antidote to apostasy.

The reality is that the Christian life is hard. Yes, there are things about it that are fantastic, wonderful, and exhilarating. And there is no other life you want to live. But, at the same time, it is hard. Sometimes we just want to ring the bell. Our author acknowledges that to his readers, who have had a rough time of it: "You endured a hard struggle with sufferings, sometimes being publicly exposed to reproach and affliction" (**v 32-33**).

It is sometimes like that for us too—which is why we need this simple lesson: "Do not quit."

## Look Back

Just like the SEAL recruits, our author first tells his readers to look back to their lives right after they first professed Christ: "Recall the former days when, after you were enlightened..." (**v 32**).

The term "enlightened" means "having come to awareness." It is referring to the time when they first embraced the truth and became followers of Christ.

Why look back to that time? Because the early days of your Christian life are likely to have been a time when you had a lot of passion and excitement about your faith.

Looking back to that time can function as a warning. This is how Jesus warns the church in Ephesus in Revelation 2:4-5: "You have abandoned the love you had at first. Remember therefore from where you have fallen; repent, and do the works you did at first."

Perhaps you can look back to a time when you heard God's word taught and were thrilled by it, when you were desperate to share the gospel with your non-Christian friends, and when you walked with zeal. When you compare that to your current life, you might think, "What happened to that person?" You may feel that once you were running well but that now you're stumbling and falling.

But in Philippians 1:6 Paul says, "I am sure of this, that he who began a good work in you will bring it to completion at the day of Jesus Christ." God finishes what he starts. So, looking back is not only a way of warning yourself about how far you have fallen but also a reason for encouragement. If you were running well to begin with, you can run well again—because God has promised to bring his good work in you to completion.

It's not all that different than what a married couple might do when their relationship hits a rough patch. They might look back at their wedding pictures to remind themselves of why they love one another and to remember how much zeal and passion there once was in their relationship. Looking back reminds them that what they had was real, and so it is worth their perseverance.

The author knows a lot about the people he is writing to, and so he takes them down memory lane to point out a few things about the way they used to be—laying out proofs that God really was at work in their lives. He appeals to three categories of evidence that we can all use when we look back to see how Christ has changed and used us.

The first kind of evidence is willingness to endure suffering.

The writer's original readers have "endured a hard struggle with sufferings, sometimes being publicly exposed to reproach and affliction" (Hebrews **10:32-33**). They even "joyfully accepted the plundering of [their] property" (**v 34**). Holding fast to their faith was worth all that.

Our author has watched how his readers endured suffering in the past and now calls them to remember it. *Don't ring that bell,* he is saying. *Look how far you have come.*

Loving others is the second piece of evidence that demonstrates God is at work in a person's life. The original readers not only suffered reproach and affliction on their own account but were also "partners with those so treated. For you had compassion on those in prison" (**v 33**).

Early Christians spent a lot of time visiting people who had been imprisoned for their faith. These prisoners depended on their brothers and sisters in Christ to bring them food and look after them while they were locked up.

John 4:12 says, "If we love one another, God abides in us." Love is the hallmark of the work of God in someone's life: looking outside themselves, giving to others, and loving others. This is what the first readers of Hebrews had done.

Perhaps you have read this passage and wonder whether you are really saved. You may realize that you have not loved people as well as you should.

But understand that falling short is not evidence that you are not a Christian. We all fall short. If you look at your life and see no fruit at all, you need to be concerned. But if you are a Christian, there will be ways in which God is at work in you. Striving toward loving people is one of those areas.

A third piece of evidence is the state of your heart—the joy within you.

Think back to when you were first a believer. I would imagine that if you were looking for one word to sum up what was in your heart, you might choose the word "joy." Joy is evidence of a heart filled with God's Spirit. It is one of the fruits of the Spirit in Galatians 5.

Life does not feel that way all of the time, of course. If you are not full of joy now, that does not mean that you are not saved. The author's whole point is to urge us to go back and remember what used to be true, even if it is not so now. He is reminding the Hebrews of their former joy.

His readers "joyfully accepted the plundering of [their] property," because they knew that they had "a better possession and an abiding one" (Hebrews **10:34**).

How many of us would joyfully accept the plundering of our property? If I came home one day and found my house had been flattened, I would probably crumble to the ground too. I think most of us would. Yet the Hebrews endured that joyfully, because they had a better possession.

I wish, I hope, I would be able to look at my house completely destroyed and say, "My home in heaven is untouched." God has a place for us which cannot be destroyed and which cannot rust away (Matthew 6:20).

If we are honest, it is not easy to have that perspective. Losing things *is* bad, and it is justifiable to be upset at the loss of possessions; but loss can also be an opportunity to see the true state of your heart—and an opportunity to see who God really is. You do not get that chance if you have everything. Sometimes something has to be taken away.

And that is what the readers of Hebrews experienced. They had it all taken away, and they realized that Christ was above all. That's certainly evidence that God was at work in them and among them.

Some families make marks on a wall or door frame to track their children's growth. Looking back as Hebrews **10:32-34** describes here is a way of tracking growth spiritually—a way of saying, "Here's where God did that in my life. Here's where God looked after me." That is a huge encouragement as we keep growing.

This section concludes with a simple exhortation: "Therefore"— given all that you endured—"do not throw away your confidence" (**v 35**). Don't give up on your faith, if you have come this far. Looking back motivates you to keep going.

But then our author transitions immediately to his next point: we should also keep going because of "a great reward." There is a paradox here. We look back in order to look forward. So, now we transition to the great blessings that await us.

## Look Forward

The Christian life is about endurance—making it to the end.

"You have need of endurance," our author tells us, "so that when you have done the will of God you may receive what is promised" (**v 36**).

There are two kinds of runners: sprinters and long-distance runners. Sprinting is over in a matter of seconds. You go as fast as you possibly can for a short amount of time. But with endurance running, you have to keep running for the long haul.

I have watched Ironman competitions, where you have to swim, bike, and run. Nine hours after the start it's dark, and there are people *still* coming across the finish line. But these people aren't thinking, "I didn't finish with a world-record time, so I'll quit." No, they're thinking, "No matter what I do, I'm finishing this race."

The Christian life is like that. This is not to suggest that God is unconcerned about how we live, as if the quality of our Christian lives doesn't matter. Rather it is a simple reminder that the Christian life is forward-looking. We need to keep our eye on the ultimate goal, the finish line. And like those Ironman athletes, we will never quit until we cross it.

> This is the greatest reward of all: we will spend eternity with our Savior, face to face.

For this reason, our author points us again to the finish line. You are to run "so that ... you may receive what has been promised" (**v 36**). This is a reference to that "great reward" that awaits us.

What would it do to our lives if we thought more about the reward we are promised in Christ? We so easily become jaded and stop thinking about it. Or perhaps we become complacent—life here is nice, so there is no reason to think about looking forward. We don't think about rewards because we don't have to; we are not compelled to. That is why suffering in one sense can be a great blessing spiritually.

This reminds me of a **Puritan** writer by the name of Richard Baxter. Late in his life he grew very ill. Yet, he did something remarkable to keep himself motivated: he spent 30 minutes each day meditating on the glories of heaven. When he thought through what heaven would be like and the reward and glory that await, it completely revolutionized his life—transforming his joy, his passion, his love, and his perspective on everything. Eventually his thoughts on heaven formed one of his most famous books, *The Saints' Everlasting Rest.*

Pondering our reward in heaven is transformative for the present. Too often, we do not think about it. We don't reflect on it. We don't meditate on it. We don't memorize Scripture on it. But this passage is reminding us to look forward to a great reward.

Do not mistake what this passage is saying: this reward is not something we earn, and it is not money or other material wealth. The great reward is the gift of eternal life in heaven—where there will be no more pain and no more tears. There will be a new order of things. There will be fellowship with other believers—those who came ahead of us and those who come beside us.

But the greatest reward of all is Christ himself. What we are looking forward to is a person. We will spend eternity with our Savior, face to face.

That is why **verse 37** speaks about the second coming. "Yet a little while, and the coming one will come and will not delay." This is a quotation from Habakkuk 2:3-4. When Jesus comes back again, those who "live by faith" will be rewarded.

The quotation continues with a warning: "If he shrinks back, my soul has no pleasure in him" (Hebrews **10:38**). In other words, if you give up and reject Christ—if you ring the bell—then you will not gain the reward of being with him in heaven.

But in the final verse of the chapter, we return to optimism. After looking back at his readers' lives and the way God has worked in them so far, and after encouraging them to look forward to the present, our author has the confidence to say, "We are not of those who shrink back and are destroyed, but of those who have faith and preserve their souls" (**v 39**).

*Here is what I know about you,* the author is saying to his readers. *I know you are going to make it. I know you are not going to give up.*

He has great hope for his audience—that they will listen to his encouragements, heed his warnings, understand his theology, and wholeheartedly obey his instructions to draw near to God.

In short, he's saying to his audience: *You are the kind of people who live by faith.* And that will be the topic of his next chapter.

## Questions for reflection

1. When you look back to your early years as a believer, what encourages you?

2. Why is it so important to remember that endurance and perseverance are keys to the Christian life? How should that affect you today?

3. How would your life be different if you were motivated by the joy of heaven rather than only by fear of judgment?

# 10. CONFIDENT FAITH, RADICAL OBEDIENCE

While our modern world might distance itself from many Christian concepts, *faith* is not one of them. Our world loves to talk about faith (think Oprah Winfrey), and even sing about faith (think George Michael). As far as our culture is concerned, faith is a feeling—a positive outlook on life. Faith is great.

But what is that rosy view of faith based on? Often it means having faith in yourself. It is about becoming who you're really meant to be.

That idea does not stand up to scrutiny. Faith becomes just something that you conjure up in yourself. It is something to add to the list of things that we need to do in order to be successful. And it doesn't work with the reality of what people are like. After all, if true faith is all about looking inward and seeing how great I am, that is not such good news. I'm a mess!

The biblical definition of faith is radically different. It is not about being a positive thinker. Instead we are called to take our trust and place it in something outside ourselves.

Hebrews 11 is sometimes known as the Hall of Faith. It takes us through many Old Testament saints and reminds us of what God can accomplish through his people when they trust him. But the key lesson is not "Go out and do great things." It is not about you or me and what we can achieve if we just have faith. Yes, it is a call to have faith;

but it is really about the object of our faith: the person we are trusting in. The main theme of Hebrews 11 is *Trust in God*.

This leads straight into **11:1**, which gives us a definition of faith.

## The Certainty of Faith

"Faith is the assurance of things hoped for, the conviction of things not seen." (**v 1**)

Faith is not just a feeling. It is not just saying, "I hope it's true." It means being certain about something. Notice the two key words in this first verse: "assurance" and "conviction." Faith is rock-solid trust that when God makes a promise, it is true and right. It is absolute assurance and confidence that God's word can be relied upon.

In our day, if you claim to be certain that your religious convictions are true, you are likely to be condemned as arrogant. You can see why: if I claim that a religious truth is really true, then that means that I think someone else's version of religion is not true. And that is not fashionable in our world today. The biblical definition of faith swims right against the tide of our culture.

Of course, a Christian is not always certain about everything. Doubt is a very normal part of the Christian life. But Christians should respond to doubt differently than non-Christians. People in our world today sometimes embrace doubt and uncertainty as things worth striving for in themselves; Christians, by contrast, believe that there are certainties, even though we may find it difficult to hold on to them. So, when we have those struggles with doubt, we fight them. We look for reassurance from God.

## The Object of Faith

So, if faith is "assurance" about something, what is it exactly that we have this assurance about? **Verse 1** highlights the two types of things that we know by faith. "Things hoped for" are things in the future that have not yet happened. "Things not seen" are things in the past—events that we were not there to see. Or, put simply, our faith is in what God *has done* and in what God *will do*.

Belief in what God has done in the past is illustrated in **verse 3**. "By faith we understand that the universe was created by the word of God, so that what is seen was not made out of things that are visible."

You were not there to see God make the world. Nobody was. So how do you know he did it? You have to believe it by faith.

There are many other things in the past that we take on faith because we weren't there to see them. Were you there to watch Noah build the ark? Were you there to see Moses lead the way through the Red Sea? Were you there to see Jesus die on the cross? These are all events that we embrace as true—by faith.

Is that faith groundless? Absolutely not. We have tremendous historical evidence that confirms what we know by faith. The stories we read about in the Bible are historical, and we can trust the books of the Bible as reliable. When we say we have faith in something we cannot see, we don't mean that there are no good reasons to believe in it. It just means that we were not there to see it with our eyes.

Yet faith is not just about what God has already done but also about what God will do in the future: "things hoped for." You cannot know about the future just by empirical evidence. You cannot see it. You have to trust God about what it will be like.

In the context of the book of Hebrews—particularly the later sections of chapter 11—there is no doubt that what our author is alluding to is the second coming of Christ. We look back to creation with faith in what we have not seen; but we also look forward with hope to a new creation, when Jesus will return to set all things right.

We have to trust God with what is coming. We have to believe that Jesus is real and that he is coming back. We also have to trust him with our lives and our own futures. There are probably a lot of things in your life that you are worried about, and it's easy to wish you could see the future. But that is exactly where faith kicks in. You hope for what you do not see (Romans 8:24-25). Part of faith is trusting that God will provide for you, walk before you, and keep his promises to you as you go.

Faith either looks back at what God has done or looks to the future at what God will do. Either way—and this is key—faith is about trusting God. It is not faith in ourselves. It's about trusting something *outside* of ourselves.

Here is where we can see what makes faith so powerful. What makes faith work is what you put your faith in, not how much of it you have. We often assume that what makes faith successful is how strong it is. But that is not true. What makes faith so powerful is the object of your faith.

I have my pilot's license, and years ago I used to fly small single-engine airplanes. Every once in a while, I'd fly down to the coast of North Carolina and just look out across the Atlantic. I would wonder, "If I just flew off toward England, how far would I get?"

Imagine that on one of those occasions, I had become absolutely convinced that my little plane could make it all the way. Regardless of how much faith I had in that little plane, it wouldn't have mattered. About an hour off the coast I would have run out of gas and had to ditch in the ocean. Even if my faith were as solid and strong as a rock, it would have been in the wrong object.

> Our faith depends on something external, not feelings and experience.

But imagine another person who is getting ready to board a 747. They are a nervous flier and they don't have much faith that this plane will really get them across the ocean. But they eventually (albeit barely) get on the plane—and of course it makes it across the ocean all the way to England. Their faith may be small and weak, but it is in the right object.

That is the essence of faith. What matters is what you're believing in. It is possible to gain a sense of certainty in our faith because it depends on something external, not on our own feelings and experience. Faith gets its assurance by focusing on its object—which for us, ultimately, is Christ.

## Faith and Favor

Hebrews **11:2** reveals that faith is the key that unlocks everything in the Christian life. It is not simply about what we believe to be true. It is also about how we relate to God and receive his favor. "By it the people of old received their commendation." We'll see the same idea picked up in **verse 6**: "Without faith it is impossible to please him."

We please God by faith. This has always been true for God's people. It is only by faith that anyone, in any time, can be considered righteous in the eyes of God.

This was Martin Luther's big discovery. He was reading through his Bible one day and came across the passage in Habakkuk which we saw quoted in Hebrews 10:37-38: "The righteous shall live by his faith" (Habakkuk 2:4; Luther was reading the quotation of this verse in Romans 1:17).

Luther had spent his whole life up to that point thinking that the way to please God was to outdo everybody around you with good works—in his case, to "out-monk" the other monks. But when he read that verse, something suddenly clicked. At that moment, Luther realized the truth: faith is the only means of salvation and the only way to please God. He wrote, "I felt that I was altogether born again and had entered paradise itself through open gates" (*Luther's Works*, Volume 34, p 337).

Of course, we must again be clear about what we mean when we say we "please" God by our faith. It is not as if faith is meritorious good work that God rewards. No, it simply means that faith is the sole means by which we receive the thing that saves: namely, Christ. And since God is pleased with Christ, he is pleased with us.

## Faith in Practice

In the following verses, our author fleshes out his definition of faith with three examples. He goes back to Genesis and picks out three saints: Abel, Enoch, and Noah. Each of these examples highlights a particular aspect of faith—and a particular lesson that we need to hear.

The first lesson is that you don't just put faith in God in a generic way; you always approach him through Christ. The story of Abel (Hebrews **11:4**) teaches us that that is how it has always been.

"By faith Abel offered to God a more acceptable sacrifice than Cain, through which he was commended as righteous, God commending him by accepting his gifts."

The story of Cain and Abel is told in Genesis 4:2-16. The two brothers both bring an offering to God. Cain brings grain or fruit, while Abel brings an animal and sheds its blood before God. God accepts Abel's sacrifice but not Cain's offering.

Since the narrative in Genesis 4 does not expressly tell us why God accepts one sacrifice and not the other, there has been disagreement among scholars about the reason. But when we look at the story from the perspective of the book of Hebrews—and the argument of the author up to this point—a good case can be made that Abel's sacrifice was approved precisely because it included the shedding of blood. After all, our author just talked extensively in chapters 9 and 10 about the necessity of blood sacrifice to rightly approach God's throne. Since the fall it has always been this way, so that "not even the first covenant was inaugurated without blood" (Hebrews 9:18).

It is possible, then, that Abel recognized this reality, and so, when he made an offering to God, he brought an animal sacrifice. Of course, an animal's blood could not take away sins. But Abel's offering foreshadowed what Christ would do. Abel enjoyed God's favor because he put his faith in the sacrifice.

You cannot approach God in just any way you want to. Cain tried that, and it did not work. You always have to approach God through the shed blood of the Savior.

The world still divides into Cains and Abels: those who approach God in their own way and those who approach God through Christ. Western society will tell you that each person gets to decide for themselves how to approach God. But the Scriptures say otherwise. In a sense, Abel's voice can still be heard today: "Though he died, he still speaks" (**11:4**). This means the lesson of Abel's life is still as applicable as ever: namely, that we must always approach God by faith through a blood sacrifice.

The second aspect of faith is found in the story of Enoch.

Enoch appears in Genesis 5:18-24. The main thing to realize about him is that he and God were close. We are told twice that he "walked with God" (v 22, 24). In fact, Enoch and God were so close that one day, "he was not, for God took him" (v 24). Hebrews **11:5** spells out what for us this means: "By faith Enoch was taken up so that he should not see death." Enoch went to heaven without having died an earthly death.

The reason is that "before he was taken he was commended as having pleased God. And without faith it is impossible to please him" (**v 5-6**). Like Abel, Enoch pleased God by faith.

Faith is inherently relational. It is the means by which we relate to God personally. The Christian life is not simply knowing things about God—assenting to intellectual truths. It is a personal, daily relationship with God.

This is what **verse 6** is getting at: "Without faith it is impossible to please him, for whoever would draw near to God must believe that he exists and that he rewards those who seek him."

Of course, this faith is not just a feeling or an emotion. As we discussed above, it has an object. It is faith in Christ. We need to remember that Abel and Enoch (and the rest of those celebrated in the Hall of Faith) all put their trust in the **Messiah** who was to come. While we look back on Jesus, they looked forward to Jesus.

As we will see below, Abraham is the ultimate example of an Old Testament saint trusting in Jesus. Jesus tells us plainly, "Abraham rejoiced that he would see my day. He saw it and was glad" (John 8:56). And when Paul was searching for a classic example of **justification** by faith alone, he didn't pick a New Testament believer. In Romans 4:1-12, he picks Abraham!

While faith starts with the cross, it doesn't stop there. It continues on as a personal relationship with the Lord. God is not just a philosophical concept. He is a real person with whom you can have a relationship. Faith means drawing near to God and seeking him.

Does your faith lead to spending time in prayer and Bible reading on a regular basis? Are you investing time with God as you would with any other person? Faith is not just about ritual; it is not just about ideas in our head. It is about a personal relationship with God. Enoch illustrates that perfectly.

Third, we come to Noah, who teaches us that faith leads to obedience, even when things don't make sense.

Noah was "warned by God concerning events as yet unseen" (Hebrews **11:7**). If faith is "the conviction of things not seen," there are few better examples than Noah. God gave him a command which made no sense on a human level—to build a boat, over five hundred feet long and over fifty feet high, in the middle of the dry land—and asked for his obedience. Noah obeyed "in reverent fear"—and saved his family.

Faith leads us into radical obedience, even in the face of things that do not make sense. The essence of faith is looking outside your own understanding and deciding to obey because you trust that God is right.

Indeed, we are told that by this radical obedience, Noah "condemned the world" (**v 7**). In other words, it showed that he believed God and not the hollow promises of the culture in his day. Since the rest of the world rejected God's warning, they were left only with judgment.

But don't think Noah was approved by God simply because of his obedience. No, the passage tells us plainly that Noah "became an "heir of the righteousness *that comes by faith*." In other words, his righteous standing before God was not acquired on the basis of his good works but on his trust in a future savior. The same was true of Abraham. Paul tells us that "Abraham believed God, and it was counted to him as righteousness" (Romans 4:3).

Even so, Noah's faith led to amazing acts of obedience. And seeing such obedience should be an encouragement to us. At our core, we all tend to be skeptics when it comes to radical obedience. We tend to think that nobody really does obey God that way; it is not possible. But Hebrews 11 shows us that our skepticism is unwarranted. It is a long list of people who radically obeyed God when doing so made no earthly sense. Obedience *is* possible—but only by faith.

## Questions for reflection

1. Did you have any misconceptions or misunderstandings about faith before reading this chapter? How does this passage help clarify what faith really is?

2. Why do you think we are always tempted to make good works the grounds for our relationship with God rather than faith?

3. Which of the three lessons about faith (Abel, Enoch, and Noah) do you need to hear the most today? How does that lesson encourage or challenge you?

## PART TWO

"There's no place like home."

Famously uttered by Dorothy in *The Wizard of Oz*, this may be one of the best-known lines in cinematic history. It has survived the test of time not just because it was spoken in a popular film, but because we all know it's true. There really is something special about being home, where things are safe and familiar.

But what if God asked you to leave your comfortable home? What if he asked you to leave and didn't even tell you where you were going or what it would be like once you got there? Would you go?

That's precisely the situation in which Abraham found himself. He was faced with circumstances that would require radical obedience. And this would not be the only time.

Hebrews **11:8-22** reviews Abraham's great legacy. And here's the big lesson we learn from his life: *radical obedience requires radical beliefs*. Great deeds are not accomplished just by effort or will power. No, they flow naturally from what we believe. They are born out of faith.

## A Better Home

Hebrews **11:8** rehearses the events of Genesis 12:1, when God called Abraham to leave his home and journey to a foreign land. He was "to go out to a place that he was to receive as an inheritance." But here's the problem: Abraham didn't know "where he was going"!

Of course, God promised that this plot of land—the land of Canaan—would one day become the inheritance of Abraham's many descendants. But Abraham did not get to see that day. On the contrary, "he went to live in the land of promise, as in a foreign land, living in tents" (Hebrews **11:9**).

Even so, we read that Abraham did not resist or delay his departure. He did not complain or make excuses. Instead, "Abraham obeyed when he was called" (**v 8**). This is an echo of Genesis 12:4: "So **Abram** went, as the Lord had told him."

So, what allowed Abraham to carry out such an amazing act of obedience? We are told that he did it "by faith"—the refrain repeated throughout this entire chapter. Abraham believed something that allowed him to obey. Hebrews **11:10** tells us what that was: "For he was looking forward to the city that has foundations, whose designer and builder is God."

This is incredible. We might have expected the text to say that Abraham obeyed because he couldn't wait to enjoy this new land that God had promised him. But instead we are told that Abraham obeyed because he was "looking forward" to a different land altogether! He was willing to leave his home because his hope was in a future city that was eternal, not temporary—a heavenly city, not an earthly one. A city with "foundations" is a permanent city. Instead of just "living in tents" (**v 9**), one day Abraham would have a dwelling that is unshakable (12:28).

Abraham knew the promised land of Canaan was not his ultimate reward. We see here an echo of the themes in Hebrews 3 and 4: God's "rest" was never just a physical plot of land somewhere. The ultimate rest is (and always was) our future heavenly home.

## A Better People

Abraham was willing to leave his home because he trusted in God's promise. But this was not the only time his faith would be tested. God made another promise to Abraham—and this one was also difficult to believe. God promised that Abraham's descendants would be like "the stars of heaven and as the sand that is on the seashore" (Genesis 22:17).

There was just one little problem. Sarah was "past the age" (Hebrews **11:11**) of conceiving a child. She was barren. And Abraham was so old that he was "as good as dead" (**v 12**). Indeed, this promise was so difficult to believe that at first Sarah laughed (Genesis 18:12). Even though Abraham believed God's promise (Genesis 15:6), he seemed to struggle with his own doubt at times, taking his servant Hagar and conceiving with her instead (Genesis 16:4).

But despite these initial doubts, Sarah did believe God. Hebrews **11:11** says she "received power to conceive" precisely because "she considered him faithful who had promised."

Because of the faith of both Abraham and Sarah, we are told that God did what he promised—from one man there were descendants like the "stars of heaven" and the "sand by the seashore" (**v 12**).

We should remember, however, that God's promise regarding Abraham's "offspring" is like the promise he made about the land— *it points forward to something greater.* Indeed, Paul picks up on this language in his letter to the Galatians and reminds us that "the promises were made to Abraham and to his offspring. It does not say, 'And to offsprings,' referring to many, but referring to one ... who is Christ" (Galatians 3:16).

Furthermore, it was not just Abraham's physical offspring, and not even only Christ, that God had in mind when he made the promise but the *spiritual* offspring that come through Christ. That's why Paul could make this stunning statement in Galatians a few verses later: "If you are Christ's, then you are Abraham's offspring, heirs according to promise" (3:29). This would have been mind-blowing to anyone in Paul's Jewish world. The descendants like the stars in the sky were not ultimately referring to the nation of Israel but to all who would trust in Jesus. And that means Abraham's offspring would include *all nations*, not just ethnic Israel.

Incredibly, Abraham was not looking forward to just a heavenly land but also to a heavenly people. He was looking forward to a people who were defined *by their faith*. This was precisely what God promised in the new covenant: a new people who would have the law written on their hearts (Hebrews 8:10-11; Jeremiah 31:33-34).

## A Future Hope

In Hebrews **11:13-16**, our author focuses again on the beliefs and attitudes that fueled the radical obedience of the great saints of the Old Testament, with Abraham still primarily in view. In essence, their faith was *forward looking*, anticipating that God would keep his promises in the future. After all, "these all died in faith, not having received the things promised" (**v 13**). They realized they would never in this life see the complete fulfillments of God's promise, but nevertheless "greeted them from afar."

By doing so, these saints demonstrated the core principle of faith noted at the beginning of this great chapter—Hebrews 11. Faith, by definition, is "the assurance of things hoped for, the conviction of things not seen" (**v 1**). They didn't see, but they still believed.

This forward-looking posture of faith meant that Abraham and the patriarchs did not view this world as their real home. Instead, they "acknowledged that they were strangers and exiles on the earth" (**v 13**).

This is particularly remarkable language in the case of Abraham because he actually made it to the promised land. However, even while in Canaan, Abraham considered himself a foreigner because he was still "seeking a homeland" (**v 14**). He was after "a better country, that is, a heavenly one" (**v 16**).

Once again, our author uses the word "better." As noted in the introduction, the idea that Jesus—and all that he brings in the new covenant—is better is basically the theme of the whole book. We have seen that we have a "better hope" (7:19), a "better covenant" (7:22), with "better promises" (8:6), "better sacrifices" (9:23), and a "better possession" (10:34). And now we have a "better country" (**11:16**).

In case anyone doubted that the patriarchs were interested more in a heavenly home than an earthly one, our author offers additional proof: "If they had been thinking of that land from which they had gone out, they would have had opportunity to return" (**v 15**). This is a basic appeal to logic. If the patriarchs were longing for their earthly homeland, they could have just travelled there! But instead they turned their attention to the future home that awaited them.

In short, these great saints *didn't turn back*. No doubt this would have been a challenge to the original recipients of Hebrews, which consisted of Jewish Christians tempted to return to the ways of the old covenant. The example of Abraham encourages them to look forward, not backward.

This is why we are told that "God is not ashamed to be called their God, for he has prepared for them a city" (**v 16**). Essentially, God is honoring their faith. Because they wanted to be with God, God prepares a place where they can be with him. This is an echo of **verse 6**: "[God] rewards those who seek him."

Abraham's example can be a powerful one in our modern world. Particularly in the West, most of us are affluent enough to enjoy nice homes—ones that are comfortable and safe. As a result, we can easily begin to make this world our home, forgetting that a much better one—a real and glorious one—awaits us.

In short, we've become enamored with the seen things rather than the unseen. The cure to this kind of worldliness is to change what we believe—about God and about ourselves. We need to recover our real identity as "strangers and exiles." When we remember that we are just passing through, we are less apt to place our hope in our earthly dwellings. Like Abraham, we need to consider our present homes to be like "living in tents" (**v 9**)—they are transient and temporary.

> When we remember that we are just passing through, we are less apt to place our hope in our earthly dwellings.

## The Ultimate Test

God asked Abraham to trust him in some very difficult circumstances—in leaving his home for an unknown land and in believing he would have an heir despite Sarah's barren womb. But all of that seems like just a warm-up for what was next. Abraham was "tested" by God when he was asked to do the unthinkable: to offer up his son Isaac (**v 17**; see Genesis 22:1-2).

It is hard to wrap our minds around how difficult this would have been. At the most obvious level, this boy Isaac—now probably around the age of 12 or 13—was Abraham's son. No doubt he loved him more than life itself. Beyond this, God's command seemed out of sync with his earlier promises. Remember, God had promised that Abraham would have offspring like the stars in the sky; and Isaac was the key to that promise. If Isaac died, how would God keep his promise?

Our passage acknowledges precisely this dilemma by adding two bits of information that seem superfluous. First, Hebrews **11:17** reminds us that Abraham was the one "who had received the promises" regarding his future offspring. Then **verse 18** adds a simple fact about Isaac: "… of whom it was said, 'Through Isaac shall your offspring be named'" (citing Genesis 21:12). In other words, our author wants us to feel the dilemma that Abraham felt.

In this particular story, we come face to face with one of the most common (and most difficult) ways that God tests people: *he asks us to obey him even when it doesn't make sense.* We will see this come up again later in Hebrews 11, but certainly Abraham faced one of the most challenging versions of this test. To give up your own child—for what seems like no good reason—might be the hardest test anyone could ever face.

Incredibly, Abraham obeys again. And he obeys immediately. We are told simply that he offered up Isaac (**v 17**). There were no complaints, no questions, no resistance. The immediate nature of Abraham's obedience is particularly clear in the original Genesis account, where we read that Abraham, after hearing God's command, "rose early in the morning" to do it (Genesis 22:3).

Of course, at this point there is an obvious, burning question: how? How could any man obey like this under such difficult circumstances?

It is here that our author returns again to the theme of the chapter: Abraham's obedience *flowed from his faith*. It was empowered by what he believed. And what did he believe? **Verse 19** tells us something amazing: "He considered that God was able even to raise him [Isaac] from the dead." Abraham was so sure that God would keep his promise that he figured that God must intend to do a miracle—to bring Isaac back to life if necessary.

Even though everyone would have known how the story ended, the author is keen to say it: Abraham "did receive him back." Isaac was not raised from the dead literally, but he was "figuratively" raised, meaning that he escaped death. And he escaped death because a substitute was made for him: "a ram, caught in a thicket by his horns" (Genesis 22:13). Isaac lived because another died. His blood was spared because the blood of another was shed.

What a fitting picture of Christ in the book of Hebrews. Our author has been focused on how bloodshed is needed for **absolution**. The story of Abraham and Isaac is a perfect picture of this reality—a picture of the gospel message.

One day God, like Abraham, would put into action his plan to sacrifice his one and only Son. But there would be a big difference. This time, no one would come to the rescue. This time there would be no angel sent to intervene, as was done for Isaac. In the case of the Son of God, there would be no reprieve. He would actually die. And he would actually be raised from the dead.

## The Legacy of Faith

Since Abraham was so faithful, it is no surprise that his offspring exhibited that same faith. In Hebrews **11:20-22**, our author turns to the next few generations, showing that they too were forward-looking people who trusted in God's promises.

We are reminded in **verse 20** that Isaac bestowed "future blessings" on his sons, Jacob and Esau (Genesis 27:27-29, 39-40). Yes, Jacob obtained his blessing deceitfully through trickery. Nevertheless, Isaac's faith was evident; he trusted that God would keep his promises to bless the "offspring" of Abraham, which included these two sons.

Even though Jacob had lied to his father, he was still a man of faith, and the **covenant line** continued through him, not Esau. It is a reminder again that God sometimes works through the unlikeliest of people. Some seem as if they would believe and yet do not, and some seem as if they would never believe, and yet, by God's grace, they do.

Jacob's faith is also on display when he blesses the next generation. In his case, we are told that he "blessed each of the sons of Joseph" (Hebrews **11:21**), a reference to the scene of Jacob on his deathbed in Genesis 48:17-20. In addition to the blessing, Jacob's faith is also exhibited by the fact that he bowed in worship "over the head of his staff." (Our author relies on the Greek version of the Old Testament here, whereas the Hebrew mentions "head of his bed.") This is actually a separate scene (Genesis 47:31; the NASB, a more literal translation, makes that clearer.)

Since Joseph has just been mentioned, our author finishes this section by talking about how **Joseph**'s faith was displayed at the end of his life when he "made mention of the exodus of the Israelites and gave directions concerning his bones" (Hebrews **11:22**). This refers to Genesis 50:24-25, where Joseph reminded his brothers that God's promise to give his people the land of Canaan would be fulfilled. Someday, they would be delivered from Egypt, and he wanted them to take his bones with them.

Joseph's story is a good place to end this section because his confident faith is palpable in his final words. He *really* did believe that God would do what he promised. In fact, you will notice that these last three examples of faith all pertain to what these patriarchs said on their deathbed. Facing death is the real test of one's faith. It is the moment when we realize—more than at any other moment, perhaps—that this earthly world is not our real home.

In each case—Isaac, Jacob, and Joseph—these Old Testament saints showed that they were really longing for a heavenly home—one "whose designer and builder is God" (Hebrews **11:10**).

## Questions for reflection

1. In what ways do you see your heart being drawn away from the city of God?

2. Do the promise of heaven and the faithfulness of God give you the courage to live differently in this world? How?

3. How does the faithfulness of Abraham, and all of the saints who died in faith before you, give you hope and encouragement in your current situation?

# 11. THE MARKS OF TRUE FAITH

As you look at the Hall of Faith, you may wonder, "What about my faith? Am I a person who would do these things? Do I really trust God?"

What I want to suggest as we look at this chapter's final section is that we see several things that are key marks of people of faith. The author draws our attention to a series of things that faith does in your life.

Faith is the cure for our drifting hearts; without it, we drift further and further away from God. So, as you read through the rest of Hebrews 11, think to yourself, in which of these categories am I doing well, and in which am I not?

## Faith Does Not Fear Man

As our author marches through the Hall of Faith, he turns his attention to another major figure in Israel's history: Moses. Various aspects of his life are addressed in **11:23-29**.

Naturally, we begin with the remarkable story of Moses' birth. Pharaoh had issued an order that all male Hebrew babies should be killed—cast into the Nile and drowned (Exodus 1:22). But Moses' parents refused to follow the order. By faith, they hid the baby for three months because "they were not afraid of the king's edict" (Hebrews **11:23**).

We see here the first quality of faith: namely, that it empowers us to put away our fears and to do what is right. Pharaoh would have been an intimidating and fearful figure; to defy him would require serious resolve. But faith says we obey God and not men (see Acts 5:29).

Skipping down a few verses, we see that Moses had the same faith as his parents, so that he also was not afraid of Pharaoh. Hebrews **11:27**: "By faith he left Egypt, *not being afraid* of the anger of the king." What allowed Moses to overcome his fear of Pharaoh? We are told that he "endured as seeing him who is invisible." Moses believed there was someone greater than Pharaoh, who would protect and deliver his people: the "invisible" God of the universe.

And that is exactly what God did. He delivered Moses and the Israelites out of the hands of angry Pharaoh, and he did it by sending the **"Destroyer of the firstborn" (v 28)** into the land of Egypt. Moses and Israelites were protected by the fact that they "sprinkled the blood" of the Passover on their doorposts—another picture of the great sacrifice that Christ would make as the "Lamb of God" (John 1:29).

In short, Moses overcame his fear of Pharaoh by another, greater fear—the fear of the living God, who could send a "Destroyer" in judgment. One fear drove out the other. "The fear of man lays a snare, but whoever trusts in the LORD is safe" (Proverbs 29:25).

## Faith Says No to the World

After Moses' parents placed their baby in a basket, God's sovereign purpose was made evident: the child was found by the daughter of Pharaoh. As a result, his life was dramatically changed in terms of worldly comforts. He was *powerful*: being adopted by Pharaoh's daughter (Hebrews **11:24**) meant he was essentially the grandson of Pharaoh. That was the height of status and prestige. He was *wealthy*, having access to the "treasures of Egypt" (**v 26**). There were also *pleasures* available to him—"the fleeting pleasures of sin" (**v 25**). Such sin might have included a number of different things— perhaps greed, perhaps the temptation to lord it over others, or perhaps sexual pleasures.

This list contains everything the world says you should want. Power, wealth, pleasure—those are the things we are told to pursue. And even as Christians, we sometimes go along with that. We look out and see the wealth and status and fame that we can have: the comforts, the luxuries, the pleasures. There is a side of us that thinks, "That looks really good."

The scene is set up so that we can see that Moses had it all. But the amazing thing—and the thing our author wants us to focus on—is that he refused all of it.

"By faith Moses, when he was grown up, refused to be called the son of Pharaoh's daughter" (**v 24**). He decided he would rather be associated with the Israelites. He was not going to take part in the treasures of Egypt and chase the pleasures of sin. Instead he was going to join with an impoverished people and be associated with the God of Abraham.

When you see someone who has been offered so much giving it all up, you have to ask the question, "Why?" Or, to put it another way, "How?" What enabled Moses to resist all those temptations?

Of course, the answer is that he did it by faith. He believed several specific things and acted upon them.

Moses believed that the pleasures that were presented to him were fleeting (**v 25**). So much is expressed in that word; the pleasure of sin is temporary, quickly passing. The world promises a lot and delivers little. That is what Moses recognized.

Half our life is spent pursuing things that look really good on the outside but never satisfy—even good things like a restful vacation or a delicious meal. You look forward to them so much, but when you get there, you are often disappointed. How much more is that the case with sin? It may be pleasurable in the moment, but the pleasure does not last.

Do you believe what Moses believed? Or do you believe that all the things the world puts in front of you really will satisfy?

Moses also believed that real pleasure comes from following Christ.

"He considered the reproach of Christ greater wealth than the treasures of Egypt" (**v 26**). Being counted with Christ, even though it meant being scorned, was better than any pleasures that Egypt had to offer. Moses trusted in Jesus because "he was looking to the reward."

If you are really a pleasure-seeker, then you should go after the greatest pleasure imaginable: the Lord Jesus Christ himself. He is what will truly satisfy. You will be disappointed with the things of the world, but you are never going to be disappointed with Christ. He is our great reward.

> Our faith takes us into a life that is paradoxical and counterintuitive.

We should not miss the remarkable fact that our author presents Moses as a follower of Christ! Even though he lived long before Jesus, he looked ahead to the time when God would deliver his people through the *real* Passover lamb. As Jesus himself said, "If you believed Moses, you would believe me; for he wrote of me" (John 5:46).

This theme fits perfectly with what we've seen so far in the book of Hebrews. Yes, the old covenant was different in that the worship was centered on types and shadows—land, temple, sacrifices—but the essential message was the same: God's people are always saved by grace through faith in Christ.

We will have faith like Moses if we share his belief that God is ultimately going to reward those who seek him and that judgment will fall on those who do not seek him; and if we act on this belief to put ourselves under the blood of Jesus. We need to take seriously both God's judgment and his offer of salvation.

This whole section on Moses could be summed up by Jesus' teaching in Luke 17:33: "Whoever seeks to preserve his life will lose it, but whoever loses his life will keep it."

Our faith takes us into a life that is paradoxical and counterintuitive. You find life by losing it; you gain wealth by refusing to seek it;

and you find it all in Christ. The way up is down. Do not try to glorify yourself and seek the pleasures of the world; go down, humble yourself, pursue Christ. When you do, you'll find the greatest pleasure imaginable in him.

## Faith Believes Even When Things Don't Make Sense

Let's be honest: sometimes obedience to God does not seem to make sense. We see this throughout the Bible, and throughout life. It is not unusual for a Christian to say, "I know God has asked me to do this because he is clear in his word. But I don't understand how that's going to lead to something good."

This happens in the church all the time. For example, someone may say, "I want to marry this person, even though they're not a Christian." I tell them that the Bible is very clear that Christians should only marry other believers (2 Corinthians 6:14). They respond, "Yes, but I don't see how that can be a good thing. I really love this person." They know God has told them not to do it, but that does not make sense to them. They want to follow their own desires because that is where they think the path of life is.

God has a long history of asking people to do things that just do not fit with our human wisdom. That may not be comforting to you! But it is good news because God's way always proves to be better. We see three of these stories in Hebrews **11:29-31**.

The first is the story of the Red Sea. When God took his people out of Egypt, he literally guided them to a dead end. The sea was ahead of them, and Pharaoh was behind them. They were trapped between a rock and a hard place. On a human level, it did not make sense.

Of course, you know the outcome: "The people crossed the Red Sea as on dry land" (**v 29**). But in that moment, as they reached the sea, not yet knowing what was going to happen, they must have been asking God, *What were you thinking?*

But, as events unfolded, God's plan became more obvious. He intentionally led the Israelites to this dead end so that he could display his power and glory over Egypt and on behalf of Israel. Think about it: the Israelites crossed safely, "but the Egyptians, when they attempted to do the same, were drowned" (**v 29**). The contrast made a big point: don't fight against the God of Israel.

The second story is the conquering of Jericho. This was a strong city surrounded by big walls. But instead of telling the Israelites to attack or lay siege—something any normal army would do—God gave them unexpected, even bizarre, instructions. They were to march around the city for seven days, and on the seventh day to blow trumpets and shout (Joshua 6).

Wouldn't it have been better to try to scale the walls or burn them down? Was there not a better strategy? No: "By faith the walls of Jericho fell down after they had been encircled for seven days" (Hebrews **11:30**). The people went ahead and obeyed God by faith. And the walls fell.

The story of Rahab comes third. We are rewinding the story now; Rahab was an inhabitant of Jericho before it fell. Spies were sent into the city to scope it out, and Rahab decided to help them to hide and then to escape safely (Joshua 2). Talk about counterintuitive! Rahab could easily have turned in the spies. But instead she hid them, throwing in her lot with this ragtag army of Israel.

Why would she do this? Because Rahab knew where God's favor lay. She said to the spies, "I know that the LORD has given you the land" (Joshua 2:9). And because she helped them, she was saved when the city was destroyed (Joshua 6:22-25). Thus, "By faith Rahab the prostitute did not perish with those who were disobedient" (Hebrews **11:31**).

Here's the point: sometimes we don't understand what God is doing until it's all over and we can look back with a new perspective. But while we're in the midst of it, all we can do is trust.

In the movie *The Karate Kid*, a boy named Daniel learns karate from a wise old man named Miyagi. But before Daniel can have a single karate lesson, Miyagi tells him to wax his cars. Next he is asked to paint his fence, sand his decking, and even paint his house. Days later, exhausted and frustrated, Daniel eventually erupts, accusing Miyagi of being a cheat and a scammer. He came to learn karate; why is he doing all this work? But then Miyagi starts throwing punches at him, and Daniel finds he can block them. It turns out that in slaving over all these chores, he has been learning karate moves the whole time.

It is like this with God. In story after story, God is saying, *You have to trust me. I know it doesn't make sense right now, but if you trust me, it will work out in the end.*

Why does God do things this way? Is he out to get us? Does he just like making us sweat? Why does he work in ways we don't understand?

One reason is so that, when the dust settles, God is the one who gets the glory.

Think of Gideon—who will be mentioned in **verse 32**. He goes to attack the Midianites with 32,000 troops, but God says, *That's too many.* God whittles down the number further and further, until Gideon has three hundred men. When this tiny force defeats the Midianites, it is abundantly clear that they could never have done it without God's help. (This story is told in Judges 7.)

Another reason why God works this way is for our benefit (as strange as that sounds). Our faith grows the most when we're forced to trust God even when it doesn't make sense. Those are the times when God stretches us, pushes us, and builds our endurance—not that different than the way a sports coach makes his players suffer through wind sprints; it can be painful, but it is for their good.

In short, our faith is seen most visibly on display when we *don't* understand. Remember, faith is "the conviction of things not seen" (Hebrews **11:1**). If we could always see and understand exactly what was happening, then it wouldn't be by faith.

## Questions for reflection

1. How would you describe your own faith today?

2. How are you struggling today with the comforts and pleasures offered by the world? How does this passage help you to be more willing to give them up?

3. What challenges do you face in which God is asking you to trust him when it doesn't make sense? How does this passage motivate you to press on in faith?

# PART TWO

## Faith Leads to Mighty Deeds

Thus far we've seen a number of things that faith does in our life. But in **verses 32-35** our author mentions yet another: *faith enables God's people to accomplish amazing things.*

We start with a list of names in **verse 32**. The first is Gideon, whom we have mentioned already. Barak was a great general under Deborah (Judges 4). Samson famously defeated the Philistines (Judges 13 – 16). Jephthah was a great warrior (Judges 11). David was God's king. Samuel and the prophets spoke for God and upheld truth.

These people, along with others not explicitly listed, accomplished mighty things. We are told in Hebrews **11:33-35** that they "conquered kingdoms" (referring to countless military victories in the lives of Gideon, Barak, Samson, Jephthah and David); "enforced justice" (this was the job of the judges, particularly Samuel); "obtained promises" (God had promised to give Israel the land of her enemies: Joshua 1:1-5; Judges 1:2); "stopped the mouths of lions" (this was done by Samson in Judges 14:6-7 and David in 1 Samuel 17:34-36); "quenched the power of fire" (likely a reference to Shadrach, Meshach, and Abednego in Daniel 3); "escaped the edge of the sword, were made strong out of weakness, became mighty in war, put foreign armies to flight" (referring to the many battles and victories won by Israel's leaders such as David, Barak, Gideon and Samson); and "women received back their dead by resurrection" (referring to miracles performed by Elijah and Elisha in 1 Kings 17:17-23 and 2 Kings 4:18-36).

As we look at the story of God's people, we realize that it is possible to obey God and do amazing things by faith—and always by grace because God is at work. These figures trusted God, and he chose to work powerfully in their lives.

And, of course, you cannot do good works alone. How did Moses, or Gideon, or any of these saints have the strength to obey? Each of them needed to be empowered by the Holy Spirit. They "were made strong out of weakness" (Hebrews **11:34**). This is proved by the example in **verse 35**: "Women received back their dead by resurrection." Raising someone from the dead is something no one could do—except God. It is by his power alone.

Like all these people, you and I need divine help. It will never work to try to obey in our own strength. But with the help of the Spirit, obedience is the inevitable result of God's grace working through us by faith. Who knows what he may accomplish through us?

## Faith Endures Suffering

After the list of amazing deeds, there is a shift in **verse 35b**: "Some were tortured." The list continues into **verses 36-38**: God's people have suffered mocking, flogging, and imprisonment in chains; they have been stoned, sawn in two, and killed with the sword. They have been clothed in unpleasant clothes; they have been destitute, afflicted, and mistreated; they have wandered around in deserts and mountains and caves.

It is not a great advert for the Christian life, is it? *Don't bother with all the pleasures of the world. Follow Jesus and have a life of persecution, poverty, and loneliness instead!*

On a human level, no one would ever sign up for that—which is exactly why it is a mark of faith. It is people of faith, who value and love Jesus more than anything, who are willing to suffer in this way.

We can connect most of the things in this list to individual stories in the Old Testament, or to traditions outside the Old Testament. Many of the prophets were "tortured" (**v 35**) or endured "mocking" (**v 36**), or "chains and imprisonment," particularly Jeremiah, the "weeping prophet," who was beaten, put in stocks, thrown in prison, and eventually cast into a cistern (Jeremiah 20:1-2; 38:6). 2 Chronicles 24:20-21 tells us that the prophet Zechariah was "stoned" (Hebrews **11:37**), and other historical sources, tell us that the prophet Isaiah may have been "sawn in two." In general, God's people were "destitute," wearing animal skins and often "afflicted and mistreated," and often went on the run in the desert or ended up hiding in caves (1 Samuel 22:1; 1 Kings 19:4).

These verses may come as a shock after all the amazing deeds listed in the previous section. But there is a vital point to note here. God does not promise that if we follow him we will have health and wealth—becoming successful or rich. There is a sad trend in **evangelicalism** today of teachers claiming that if you follow God it will make your life better in earthly ways. Of course, it is better to follow Jesus; but that does not mean bigger bank accounts or more popularity. This is not your best life now. You could be hated; you could be persecuted; you could be put in jail.

In fact, our passage states the opposite of the "health and wealth" gospel when it reminds us that "all these, though commended through their faith, did not receive what was promised" (Hebrews **11:39**). To be clear, this doesn't mean God failed to keep his promises to these Old Testament saints. It is referring to the fact that God promised to do amazing things in the distant future—things these saints would never themselves have a chance to see. And yet, even without seeing those things, they still believed God would do them.

Does that mean their faith was a waste of time? Not at all. Even though they didn't get to experience certain blessings in their own lifetime, they will experience them in the future when God finally fulfills all his promises. In this way, these saints reflect a very common pattern in Scripture: God's people may suffer in the present, but they will receive glory in the future.

In the new covenant, of course, God has "provided something better for us" (**v 40**). We have the privilege of living in a time when many of the Old Testament promises have been realized. Even so, that doesn't mean we should expect our fullest life now. Even New Testament saints should expect hardships and persecutions until Christ returns. Indeed, Paul suffered for Christ and this forced him to look to the future:

"I count everything as loss because of the surpassing worth of knowing Christ Jesus my Lord. For his sake I have suffered the loss of all things and count them as rubbish, in order that I may gain Christ and be found in him ... Forgetting what lies behind and straining forward to what lies ahead, I press on toward the goal for the prize of the upward call of God in Christ Jesus." (Philippians 3:8-9, 13-14)

If you follow God, you do not get it all now. In Christ you do get it all; but you get it on that final day when Christ looks at you and says, "Well done, good and faithful servant" (Matthew 25:23).

The question, then, is, are you ready for that? Do you have faith in the Lord Jesus Christ? Can you forget what lies behind and strain forward to what lies ahead?

That is the challenge we are offered at the start of Hebrews 12.

## The Great Race

My son loves to run—track in the spring and cross country in the fall. So, I decided to get him a book about the Scottish Olympic runner, Eric Liddell. Brought to popular attention by the film *Chariots of Fire*, Liddell was a sprinter in the 1924 Olympics who refused to compete in the 100 meters because it would have required him to run on a Sunday. Instead he ran the 400 meters and ended up winning the gold medal.

Although hailed as a hero now, Eric was not viewed as such in Great Britain when he decided not to run. He was mocked and ridiculed for his faith. Most people didn't realize that he was running a much more important race than the one in the Olympics—he was running the race of the Christian life.

That is how our author describes it in **12:1**: "Let us run with endurance the race that is set before us." Everything in **verses 1-3** wraps around this theme. We are not told to walk through the Christian life, to meander or stroll along. We are told to run. It is energetic. It involves perseverance.

Our author draws on athletic imagery from the Greco-Roman world, mentioning three things every runner needs: fans cheering you on, freedom from entanglements, and a finish line in your sights.

## Fans Cheering You On

**Verse 1a** begins with the fans: "Therefore, since we are surrounded by so great a cloud of witnesses..." All those Old Testament figures mentioned in chapter 11 are now surrounding you, watching you as you run—cheering you on.

In the crowd sits Noah, who endured much hardship and faithfully built an ark; and Enoch, who loved God intimately and walked with him; and Sarah, who trusted God's promise and received power to conceive. In the crowd sit Abraham and Moses and Rahab and all the others.

But there is something very different about this crowd. They are not there to watch you. They are there to be seen by you as you run. This encourages you about what is possible. There will be times when you think you cannot finish; you cannot push past the pain. But then you realize the stadium is filled with people who have finished the race. It can be done.

I can remember going to basketball games at the Dean Dome when I was a student at the University of North Carolina. If you looked up in the rafters, you would see the names of the greats that had gone before: Michael Jordan, James Worthy, Sam Perkins. When the players are tired or discouraged, I can imagine it is a great motivation to look up and see those names. It is a reminder that you wear the same uniform and can accomplish the same great things.

## Freedom from Entanglements

The second thing runners need is freedom from anything that will slow them down. "Let us ... lay aside every weight" (**v 1b**).

Nobody would go for a serious run in a business suit; that would slow you down. Appropriate clothing was necessary in the ancient world as well. Runners would never run in a traditional robe—it would just trip them up. They would "lay aside" such garments so they could run more freely.

And if that is true for physical running, how much more is it true for spiritual running! We need to make sure that anything that could trip us up or drag us back and ruin our race is stripped off. We need to make sure we have freedom to run as we should.

Our author applies this principle in two ways. First, we should cast off "*every* weight." The implication here is that it doesn't have to be a bad or sinful thing to need casting off. It just has to be a thing that slows you down.

There are many things that could hinder our running, even if they are not bad in and of themselves. Maybe you've been sucked into social media, and it's becoming a weight or a distraction. Maybe you're watching a lot of television or are preoccupied with sports. These things are not sinful in themselves, but the question is, are they helping you run? It is so easy to spend so much time on other things that you take yourself away from what is better.

> Jesus has entered us in the race by his grace. He will sustain us until we finish.

But the second application is more obvious: we need to strip off the "sin which clings so closely." The NIV translates this phrase particularly well: "the sin that so easily entangles." *Easily*. You do not have to work very hard to be entangled by sin. In fact, that is the default in life. If you do nothing to fight it, sin will cling to you tightly. So if you are going to run the race, you have to be proactively casting off sin.

Is there any sin you are not repenting of? Is there any sin you are holding close to yourself and not getting rid of? That is like running with a rope around you, pulling you back. You are going to end up tripping and falling.

We all make mistakes, but the key to the Christian life is to own our mistakes, repent of them, and turn from them onto a new pathway of obedience. The quickest way to ruin your Christian life is to be unrepentant about sin. We have seen repeatedly through the book of Hebrews that if you hold on to sin, you are actually in danger of not finishing the race at all.

## Focus on the Finish Line

One of the classic rules of running is that you don't look around at the runners next to you to gauge your progress. Instead, you stay laser-focused on the finish line. We too have a finish line. When we run, we should be "looking to Jesus" (**v 2**).

Waiting for us is not just another member of the Hall of Faith but "the founder and perfecter of our faith." Other translations render "founder" as "pioneer"—that is, Jesus is the one who carved the path in which we walk. He has run the race *for us*, so that we might follow in his footsteps. Thus, he can rightly be considered the "perfecter" of our faith. He brings it to completion. The upshot of using this language is that it is clear that we do not run the race in our own strength. We are in the race only because Jesus has entered us in the race by his grace. He will sustain us by that same grace until we finish.

Jesus also functions as an *example* for us to follow. There are several things we can learn from Christ's race which will encourage us as we run.

First, he ran the race with great endurance. He "endured the cross"! When you think that your race is hard, look to Christ. Crucifixion put criminals on display for the whole world to see and to mock and deride. It was as much about shame as it was about physical suffering. Yet Jesus "despis[ed] the shame." He counted this as nothing for the purpose of finishing the race for us. He endured.

He also ran "for the joy that was set before him." By running the way of the cross, Jesus was going to achieve the saving of a people for himself. That was the joy set before him: the joy of you and me being with him as his people forever. He was running to save us.

There is a paradox here. Having a hard race does not mean you cannot have joy. We tend to wish we had an easier race so we could be happier. But in the Christian life pain and joy often go together. In the midst of very deep struggle, pain, and suffering, you still find joy. Most of us want our trials and challenges to go away; we think that if we can just get rid of the hard parts of life, then joy will be ours. But that is not how it works. For Christ, joy was a result of the pain.

And so Jesus received his reward. He is now "seated at the right hand of the throne of God." He resisted temptation and sin and fleeting pleasures, and came into the presence of God with perfect righteousness. He was crowned the winner of the race.

For us, our reward is Jesus himself. He is the crown. He is going to give us himself, forever. We will be beside the throne in heaven. He will be ours. And looking forward to that reward in faith is the only way you can run the Christian race. If you have your eyes firmly fixed on Jesus, the pain in your side doesn't hurt quite so badly.

Thus our passage concludes—with a final exhortation. "Consider him … so that you may not grow weary or fainthearted" (**v 3**). Even though our race may include a lot to make us weary, we must focus on the finish line that is Jesus. Those who do so "shall run and not be weary; they shall walk and not faint" (Isaiah 40:31).

# Questions for reflection

1. Do you think you are ready if serious persecution comes your way? What can you do today to help yourself be prepared to suffer?

2. How's the Christian race going for you? How are you encouraged by Jesus' example?

3. What are some things that hinder your running today that you need to put aside, even if they are not sinful?

# 12. RUN TO ZION

I can still remember where I was when it happened. It was 1980 and the United States ice hockey team was in the Olympics playing the Soviet Union. I was in my living room and I was running around screaming my head off because, with about a minute to go, we were doing the unthinkable. Here was this pesky little group of college kids from America playing the greatest ice hockey team in the entire world. There was no chance of winning this game. And yet we were winning—with about a minute left. The commentator cried, "Do you believe in miracles?"

Then—"YES!" We had won.

Was it just through sheer blind, dumb luck that the team managed to pull it off? Of course not. A lot of it came down to the coach, Herb Brooks, and what he did with his players. Brooks knew he didn't have the best team in the world. But he became famous for his grueling fitness routines as he pushed his team right to their limits. His was a simple philosophy: we may not be the best team, but we will be the fittest. One of the reasons the US team beat the Russians is that they simply wouldn't stop skating. That was because of the training they had received.

The next section of Hebrews 12 explains how hard training helps not only in sports but also in the Christian life. The word our author uses is "discipline."

Now, let's be honest: no one likes the word "discipline." We tend to think of "discipline" as negative, while "training" sounds positive. But they are two sides of the same coin. A coach may make his team run as a *punishment* because they did something wrong.

If someone shows up late, he gives them five laps round the field. It is a correction of bad behavior. But he may also make them run to *build their endurance* in general. Later in the same training session, the whole team is running laps around the field—not because they have done anything wrong but as part of their training. If you were looking at that training session from a distance and just watching players run around the field, you wouldn't know which reason was motivating the coach. Is he disciplining them or training them? In a sense it doesn't matter. It is all to make them better runners and better members of the team.

That is the same perspective we should have on God's discipline. Sometimes he disciplines us because we do wrong things; sometimes he brings discipline just to make us better runners. It is not always clear which of these God is doing. But in a sense, it doesn't matter. We can trust in our good Father, who knows what we need. He is making us fitter and more prepared to run the race.

## The Means of God's Discipline

In **verse 4** the author acknowledges the difficulties faced by his audience. They have faced all sorts of challenges, though none of them have yet had to pay the ultimate price: "You have not yet resisted to the point of shedding your blood." Curiously, he describes the difficulties of the Christian life as a "struggle against sin." This is not talking about fighting personal sins, but it is a general way to describe the challenges and difficulties of living a life faithful to Jesus, and the persecution which that entails. We know this because he compares their experience to that of Jesus, "who endured from sinners such hostility against himself" (**v 3**).

In the following verses the author interprets this situation for them: "It is for discipline that you have to endure" (**v 7**). In other words, God has allowed this suffering as a way of training these believers.

Here we come to a core (and uncomfortable) truth about discipline: *it hurts*. God's discipline, in order to get our attention, involves things that are "painful rather than pleasant" (**v 11**). We aren't best trained by blessings but by trials.

It's not that different than the way we discipline our children. How do you keep little Johnny from running into the street? You could try giving him a popsicle every time he stays inside like he's been told; but truthfully that just doesn't work as well as disciplining him when he disobeys.

C.S. Lewis, who endured a tremendous amount of personal pain, understood this. He wrote:

"God whispers to us in our pleasures, speaks in our conscience, but shouts in our pains: it is His megaphone to rouse a deaf world." (*The Problem of Pain*, p 93)

## Disciplined As Sons

Of course, if God brings pain and difficulty into our lives as discipline, then that raises questions about what he is up to. What exactly is God trying to accomplish when he does this? Our passage offers two purposes in God's discipline.

First, God's discipline is designed to *comfort us*. Now, that will sound strange in our ears. Comfort us? Pain seems like the opposite of comfort. But it comforts us because it reminds us that we are God's "sons," his real children.

In **verse 5** our author reminds his audience: "Have you forgotten the exhortation that addresses you as sons?" Then in **verse 6** he quotes from Proverbs 3:11-12. "The Lord disciplines the one he loves, and chastises every son whom he receives."

Every parent gives that little speech to their child when they punish them: "I'm doing this because I love you." And it is usually (although sadly, not always) true. It is hard, diligent, laborious work to rightly and lovingly care for your children through discipline. It is easier not to discipline children. Good parents discipline their children because they love them; they go the extra mile to rightly and carefully discipline them. They know what is good for them, and they know that discipline keeps them on the right path.

When my son John was a toddler, he kept getting out of his crib after we put him to bed. It didn't seem like a big deal, until one day when there was a knock on the door and our neighbor was standing there holding John and telling us that he had found him in his yard. We had put John down for a nap, but he had climbed out of his crib, got out of the front door, and wandered outside near a busy street. After that, we knew we had to discipline him every time he got out of his crib. Why? Because he was our son and we loved him and wanted nothing bad to happen to him. Although his little mind couldn't understand it at the time, our discipline was directly connected to his status as our beloved child.

It is the same with the Lord. He disciplines us as an expression of love. He is saying, *You are my daughter, and I love you. You are my son, and I love you. You belong to me.*

In Hebrews **12:7-9** the author goes into this more fully. "God is treating you as sons" (**v 7**). Being disciplined actually validates the fact that you are a child of God. It shows that you really belong to him. And therefore discipline is a form of comfort. It shows you that God really cares about you.

That means that a smooth, easy life may not be the good sign you think it is. "If you are left without discipline ... then you are illegitimate children and not sons" (**v 8**). Physical comfort and ease are not necessarily a sign that God is pleased with you; in fact, they might be a sign that he is displeased. Sometimes God lets the wicked prosper and have a life of ease, at least for a time (Psalm 73). Thus, a life of ease is not necessarily the blessed life.

Likewise, a life of **trials** is not a sign that God is out to get you, any more than me disciplining my son was a sign that I was out to get him. He couldn't see the bigger picture, but the reality was that I was out to love him.

Therefore we must not "regard lightly the discipline of the Lord"

(Hebrews **12:5**). This is an interesting way of putting it. He knows that we have a tendency to push discipline aside as if it is no big deal—like teenagers rolling their eyes. *I don't need to listen to you.* Some people go through trials and even end up hating God. That is why our response is as important as the discipline itself. If we are to keep on running our race, we must respond well.

Thus, it is wise, when trials come, to ask, "Is there something I need to repent of?" There may not be anything that you are actively, stubbornly holding on to; but there may be. Not all trials are due to personal sins (John 9:3), but some trials are (John 5:14).

> A smooth, easy life may not be the good sign you think it is.

The bottom line is this: don't ignore the difficult things in your life as if they were random. You and I know that God is in control of the universe—intimately. Not a hair falls from your head that God does not know about. So we know that these things have more importance than random events. God is using all these things in your life to train you and shape you. This means we must respect God, just as we do our earthly parents (Hebrews **12:9**). When we do this, we will "live." In other words, if we pay attention to our sin and keep asking for God's help, the result will be that he strengthens us in our faith and leads us to eternal life with him.

## Disciplined for Our Good

God's discipline *changes* us. Our parents disciplined us "as it seemed best to them," but God "disciplines us for our good, that we may share his holiness" (**v 10**).

Earthly discipline is flawed, and our author acknowledges this. Earthly parents, by and large, do the best they can; but their best is not perfect. Sometimes they discipline well, but other times they blow it. They don't always time it well or do it rightly. Some people's experience of discipline as a child is only one of fear and never of love. But God is not like that. He never messes up. He always knows exactly what you need. He is always perfect in his timing. His discipline is always done precisely for the good he knows it will bring you.

**Verse 11** describes the change discipline yields: "the peaceful fruit of righteousness." God trains us so that we can be more holy and more righteous. That is what will help us to make it to the end of the race.

## Stay in the Race

A common reaction to discipline is to give up—to stop running entirely. But in **verse 12** we are encouraged to "lift [our] drooping hands and strengthen [our] weak knees."

*I know you're tired, but don't stop,* says our author. In an allusion to Proverbs 3:6, our author says, "Make straight paths for your feet" (Hebrews **12:13**). That is, stay in the lane you are running in. Do not divert from the track you are on and head towards wickedness.

The paradox is that the hard thing that makes you want to quit is the very same thing that can keep you from quitting. An athlete running painful drills can give up and disobey her trainer, but in the end that means quitting her sport altogether. Or she can persevere and run those drills, and that is what will keep her in the race. In a sense, we are always on a knife edge when it comes to God's discipline. When trials come, will we quit or will we persevere and be strengthened? It is one or the other.

We must stay on the track and run, "so that what is lame may not be put out of joint but rather be healed." Again, our author continues with the running analogy. Any disability or injury we have will be helped only if we stay on the same straight path; if we verge from the path, things will "be put out of joint."

In the following verses we see what it actually looks like to persevere in this way.

First, our author exhorts us: "Strive for peace with everyone, and for the holiness without which no one will see the Lord" (**v 14**).

Throughout the Bible, godly people are presented as pursuers of peace with their fellow man (Psalm 34:14; Matthew 5:9). That's one of the key marks of holiness.

What is particularly sobering is that this holiness is somehow necessary in order to "see the Lord." To be clear, this does not mean that you earn your way to heaven through holiness, but that if you love Jesus, holiness is the result of your commitment to him. Holiness is not the condition of salvation but the consequence of salvation. If you are not on a trajectory toward holiness, you may wonder whether you are really in the race at all. This explains why our author says we should "strive" for holiness. Even if holiness is not the grounds of our salvation, it is nonetheless something that we should pursue eagerly. Grace and godly effort are not opposed to one another.

Not only are you to keep on the path, but you have to keep others on the path too. This is the point in Hebrews **12:15**: "See to it that no one fails to obtain the grace of God." Make sure, as much as humanly possible, that no one else fails. Make sure no one else falls short. Grab your brothers and sisters and keep them running with you. That means we don't leave them behind. We pray for one another and support one another.

This is important because we are in danger of a "root of bitterness" springing up which "causes trouble, and by it many become defiled." This is an allusion to Deuteronomy 29:18, where the root of bitterness is not (as we might assume) a feeling but a *person*—someone who abandons the way of the Lord and even leads others astray. The point, then, is to be on watch for one another so that apostates don't arise and harm the body of Christ.

The author ends this passage with the example of Esau, who essentially fell out of the race. Esau's undoing was the pursuit of pleasure: he "sold his **birthright** for a single meal" (Hebrews **12:16**). He was willing to sacrifice his long-term standing for short-term pleasure. He decided to take the meal and forget about the consequences. That kept Esau from finishing the race.

Of course, Esau regretted his actions later, but "he found no chance to repent, though he sought it with tears" (**v 17**). At first glance, this passage might seem to teach that God denies a person a chance to repent, even if they wish to do so. However, the focus here is not on repentance in general, but particularly on Esau's desire to undo what he had done by giving away his birthright. Thus, the lesson is rather simple: sometimes the opportunity to turn away from your rebellion passes you by (see Hebrews 6:4-6). Pursuing short-term pleasure can have long-term consequences that cannot be undone.

The way you stay in the race is to be a pursuer of holiness. In other words, the best response to discipline is not to run from God but to run to him.

## Questions for reflection

1. How does this passage change your perception of the trials in your life? How does it affect your view of God and his purposes?

2. How are you responding to God's discipline today in both good and bad ways?

3. How is Esau's example relevant for our lives today?

# PART TWO

On October 25, 1964, defensive end Jim Marshall did something re-markable in the world of professional football. After the other team fumbled the ball, he picked it up and ran 66 yards (60m) into the end zone. While that might sound like a rather ordinary play, it's famous for one simple reason: Marshall ran in the wrong direction! He ran with all his energy and all his might into the other team's end zone.

While there's certainly a lesson here for football players, there is also a lesson for the Christian life. The issue is not just whether we are running, but whether we are running toward the right finish line. In-deed, the whole book of Hebrews has been about exactly this theme. Our author is trying to persuade his audience not to run back to the ways of the old covenant but to run forward toward Jesus Christ.

In the second half of Hebrews 12, our author uses a new image to describe these two different destinations. It is essentially a choice between two mountains: Mount Sinai, representing the old covenant, and Mount Zion, representing the new covenant.

## An Earthly Place of Fear

In **verse 18** our author begins with the mountain that Christians are not (or should not be) running toward: "You have not come to what may be touched, a blazing fire and darkness and gloom and a tem-pest." Though the name is not used, this is a clear reference to Mount Sinai, the mountain which Moses climbed in Exodus 19 and 20 to receive the Ten Commandments. It is a symbol of the entire old-cove-nant way of relating to God.

In Hebrews **12:18-21**, we learn a number of key things about the old covenant. For one, this mountain is "what may be touched"—a physical place you could go to. That was very much the nature of old-covenant worship, as we saw in earlier chapters. There was a physical temple full of things you could lay your hands on, where rituals were performed.

But that is not the most important thing the author wants you to see about Mount Sinai. What he really wants you to see is how terrifying it is.

He describes "a blazing fire and darkness and gloom and a tempest and the sound of a trumpet" (**v 18-19**). This is the storm and the earthquake and the trumpet blast which happened when the people came near to Mount Sinai in Exodus 19:16-20. It was scary. All of the people were glad that it was only Moses who had to go up that mountain!

They also heard a terrible voice "whose words made the hearers beg that no further messages be spoken to them" (Hebrews **12:19**). God spoke from the mountain and ordered that no one come near it (**v 20**; see Exodus 19:10-13). If even an animal touched the mountain, it would be struck dead.

The voice of God was so overwhelming that the people cried out to Moses, "You speak to us, and we will listen; but do not let God speak to us, lest we die" (Exodus 20:19). They could not handle the overwhelming majesty and holiness of God's own voice as it came from the mountain. Even Moses was terrified: "I tremble with fear" (Hebrews **12:21**).

This terrifying scene highlights God's holiness. God is the Lord. He is the Creator. He is not just a better version of us; he is something wholly different than us. His standard of holiness is utterly perfect. That is why, in the story of Mount Sinai, God is distant. He is not inviting the people to come close to him; he is telling them to stay away, because he is holy and they are not.

We have seen this before, in Hebrews 9 and 10. Old-covenant worship was all about barriers, expressing the single major message that God is utterly holy and people are utterly sinful.

Of course, this does not mean people were not saved under the old covenant. God arranged for a system of worship by which people would draw near to God's temple through the blood of animal sacrifices. While those sacrifices did not actually take away sin, they pointed toward the coming Savior, who would be the perfect and final sacrifice. Thus, people were saved by grace through faith in the coming Messiah.

Even so, the old covenant still emphasized God's holy distance, because Christ had not yet come. Remember Hebrews 9:8, which tells us that the restrictions around the Most Holy Place shows that "the way into the holy places is not yet opened."

If a person ran back to Sinai—as opposed to running to Christ—then they would be left with only animal sacrifices to stand between them and the holy God. And we already know that "it is impossible for the blood of bulls and goats to take away sins" (Hebrews 10:4). In effect, then, to reject Christ and return to the old covenant would be attempting to draw near to God in one's own strength and on one's own merits. This would enslave a person to law-keeping as a basis for their acceptance, which inevitably would lead to a lack of assurance and peace.

But if you are in Christ, "you have not come" to Mount Sinai (**12:18**). You can admit that you are not good enough on your own and that you need grace and forgiveness. You can stop exhausting yourself on that treadmill, and you can have peace because you know that Christ is enough, and that he has already done all that needed to be done to save you.

## The Heavenly City of Joy

If you are a Christian, Mount Sinai is not where you're going. Instead, "You have come to Mount Zion and to the city of the living God, the heavenly Jerusalem" (**v 22**).

Mount Zion was a real historical location—the hill on which Jerusalem was built and the place where God's temple was located. It was understood to be the holy mountain where God "dwelled" (Psalm 2:6; 9:11; 14:7; 20:2; 50:2; 65:1; 74:2; Isaiah 2:3; 8:18). But the earthly city of Jerusalem was never an end in and of itself. It was always pointing to something more: namely, the "heavenly Jerusalem."

We should remember John 14:2, where Jesus promises his disciples, "In my Father's house are many rooms. If it were not so, would I have told you that I go to prepare a place for you?" God has a home waiting for us: a heavenly, eternal home. That is what we are talking about here.

It is easy to get sucked into spending a huge amount of time thinking about our earthly homes. TV shows are continually calling us to redo our kitchen or build an extension. We may worry about the state of our carpets or the quality of our furniture. But we should remember that we have a far better home waiting for us. If we redecorate our earthly homes, they will be out of date again in ten years' time; if we renovate them, they will eventually decay and crumble. But our eternal home can never change or decay.

The author tells us who is there in the heavenly Jerusalem. There are "innumerable angels in festal gathering" (Hebrews **12:22**); there is also "the assembly of the firstborn who are enrolled in heaven" (**v 23**)—that is, the saints who are there to be glorified, "the spirits of the righteous made perfect."

> The thunder of the law has been hushed because Jesus has satisfied it.

That line is not accidental. Mount Sinai may remind you of how unholy you are, but Mount Zion is where you find that you have been made perfect. You have been made perfect because Christ has redeemed you and changed you. You have gained righteousness and holiness by his grace. Therefore you can come even to God, "the judge of all," in confidence.

How is it possible that the same God who was so terrifying and distant on Mount Sinai can now be satisfied and welcoming at Mount Zion? **Verse 24** has the answer. We have come "to Jesus, the mediator of a new covenant." It is the climax of all we have learned in the book of Hebrews up to this point.

Christ is there, but he is not just there: he is there as your great mediator. He is there representing you, speaking on your behalf, and standing in your place. The thunder of the law has been hushed because Jesus has satisfied it.

Next, our author invokes the blood language again from chapter 10. It is Christ's blood that allows us to be received without fear by God.

The "sprinkled blood" (**12:24**) of Jesus is better than the blood of Abel. This is another contrast between the old and new covenants. The blood of Abel cried out to God for justice (Genesis 4:10)—and so it reminds us that God upholds his holy standards by bringing judgment. But Christ's blood cries out for mercy. It says, *I have died for them. Show them grace.*

That is why the new covenant is one of joy and celebration: a "festal gathering" (Hebrews **12:22**). It is a covenant of complete, unmerited mercy.

The hymnwriter John Newton—who, as a former slave trader, knew what it meant to be a terrible sinner and to find undeserved forgiveness—wrote lines that summarize this passage well.

*Let us love and sing and wonder,*
*Let us praise the Savior's name.*
*He has hushed the law's loud thunder,*
*He has quenched Mount Sinai's flame.*
*He has washed us with his blood;*
*He has brought us nigh to God.*

This song reminds us of what mountain we have come to. Do not live as if you are running to Sinai, where the thunder is loud and the fire represents God's holy presence. Run instead to Zion, where Christ has enabled us to draw near.

## Being Unshakable

Have you ever had an experience in your life where you ignored a warning but later you wished you had listened?

The 2019 film *The Challenger Disaster* details the events leading up to the explosion of the NASA Space Shuttle Challenger shortly after launch in January 1986. It tells the story of an engineer who warned NASA not to launch the shuttle that day because he knew that the O-rings, which sealed the joints in Challenger's rocket boosters, were not certified for use in cold weather. It was a freezing cold day, and essentially the engineer said, "Don't launch." But he was ignored. NASA ignored a warning they should have listened to, and the result was that seven astronauts died.

In **verse 25**, we are given a warning that we must listen to if we value our lives: "See that you do not refuse him who is speaking." Throughout Hebrews, our author has been clear that God has "spoken to us by his Son" (1:2), and that this saving message should not be ignored.

Why? Because if it is ignored, judgment will follow. To demonstrate this, our author reminds us that the Israelites at Mount Sinai, despite all the frightening sights and sounds, "refused him who warned them on earth." As a result, they "did not escape" God's judgment. Then he makes an argument from the lesser to the greater—something that appears elsewhere in the book (Hebrews 2:1-4; 10:28-29). If God held people accountable when warned on earth, "much less will we escape if we reject him who warns from heaven."

The argument here is a compelling one. The old covenant is "earthly," and yet God still held people accountable for following it. The new covenant is "heavenly," and thus we should expect even more that God would hold people responsible for following it.

To drive his point home, our author contrasts the "shaking" caused by the two covenants. Yes, God's voice "shook the earth" (**12:26**) at Mount Sinai (see Exodus 19:18). But under the new covenant there will be a greater "shaking"—that is, a greater judgment. One day in the future, God's voice "will shake not only the earth but also the heavens," a citation of Haggai 2:6. In the book of Haggai, the shaking is a picture of God's promise to judge the nations. Our author sees that promise being fulfilled ultimately in the new covenant under Christ—he will be the judge of all the world when he returns.

When Christ returns to "shake" the world, that is the moment when he will sift eternal things from temporal things. No doubt, this is a reference to the creation of a new heavens and earth, when "the things that have been made" (Hebrews **12:27**) will be transformed (see Isaiah 65 – 66; Hebrews 1:10; 2 Peter 3:10). In fact, just as Hebrews mentions the "heavenly Jerusalem" (**12:22**), so the book of Revelation describes the new heavens and new earth as involving a new Jerusalem coming down from heaven (Revelation 21:4).

The only things that will survive this monumental transition are "things that cannot be shaken" (Hebrews **12:27**): that is things that pertain to God's "kingdom" (**v 28**). All earthly kingdoms, all worldly powers and authorities will be defeated and overthrown. Only what is done for Christ is eternal and unshakable (see 1 Corinthians 3:13-14).

So what should be our response to the good news that we have a "kingdom that cannot be shaken"? We are called to do the two things that God's people are always called to do: give thanks and offer worship. First, we are told, "Let us be grateful." Thankfulness is the mark of the believer (Ephesians 5:20; Colossians 3:15-16; 1 Thessalonians 5:18) and lack of thankfulness the mark of the unbeliever (Romans 1:21).

Second, we are told, "Let us offer to God acceptable worship." It is noteworthy that worship follows thankfulness because the latter naturally leads to the former. It is really hard to worship if you are not grateful. If you go through life thinking you got the short end of the stick, then worship will not come easy. But when you read a passage like this, you realize that there is no short end of the stick here. You have come to Mount Zion and Christ—the very best place to be. It is by grasping this extraordinary grace that you can worship with gratitude.

This worship is given "with reverence and awe, for our God is a consuming fire" (**v 28-29**).

What an amazing way to end the chapter. When was the last time you heard a sermon end with the words "Don't forget, your God is a consuming fire"? Truthfully, most of us today do not want to talk about that. But we must. It is only if God is a consuming fire—only if he is holy—that his provision of a way to draw near to him is such good news.

We are not just praising someone a little bit bigger than ourselves or a little bit better than ourselves. We are worshiping the Lord of the universe—a Lord who is "holy, holy, holy" (Isaiah 6:3). Although our worship is joyful like the festal gathering of the angels (Hebrews **12:22**), it should also have gravity. Those two things seem incompatible, and for sinners they would be if it were not for Jesus. But in him the holiness of God and the joy of being in his presence are brought together. In Christ alone your sins are dealt with completely, and when he comes again, you will not be shaken. When you worship the Son, worship in the light of that fact.

## Questions for reflection

1. Do you sometimes live the Christian life as if you are under the old covenant? How does this passage change your outlook?

2. What excites or encourages you about the heavenly Jerusalem? How does knowing about the new creation help you better run the race?

3. How might a passage like this change the way you worship?

# 13. PLEASING TO GOD

It is time to get down to brass tacks. What does all the theology we have covered in the previous chapters actually look like in day-to-day life? In his final section the writer to the Hebrews covers some core aspects of how to live a holy life.

In Hebrews **13:1-6** we see that there are two ways to think of this. First, a Christian should be outwardly focused, looking to care for those around them. Second, a Christian should look inwardly at his or her own life, faith, and morality. Both the external and the internal are important.

## Brotherly Love

The chapter begins with a broad statement in **verse 1**: "Let brotherly love continue." This is the umbrella thought, the big-picture idea for how and why we look out for those around us and not just for ourselves: the concept of brotherly love.

The Greek word is *philadelphia*, which combines two words: *philo*, meaning "love," and *adelphos*, meaning "brother." The NIV translates this verse as "Keep on loving one another as brothers and sisters." That translation captures the essence of why we love. We do it because we are like brothers and sisters to one another.

Lurking behind this exhortation is this reality: that in Christ we are brothers and sisters. Believers are linked together because of Christ. We have a bond that is even stronger and tighter than biological bonds.

In Matthew 12:46-50, Jesus is teaching in a crowded room and someone comes in with the news that his brothers and mother are outside wanting to talk to him. Jesus replies, "Who is my mother, and who are my brothers?" Then he goes on, "Whoever does the will of my Father in heaven is my brother and sister and mother." He makes it clear that being spiritually related is more important than being biologically related.

This is our author's starting point. The word *philadelphia*, "brotherly love," highlights the reality that the first step to being loving is to love those in your spiritual family. Jesus said in John 13:35, "By this all people will know that you are my disciples, if you have love for one another." He did not say, *if you love everybody in the world*. The mark of a disciple is loving your spiritual siblings. Clearly, we do need to love unbelievers too! But that is not where love begins.

Brotherly love is the umbrella concept; how does it work out concretely? In Hebrews **13:2-3** our author gives two simple examples.

## Showing Hospitality

Here is the first example of brotherly love: "Do not neglect to show hospitality to strangers" (**v 2**).

Hospitality has always been one of the hallmarks of Christian communities. It was especially important in the early church, which was very mission-oriented. Even though travel could be dangerous and difficult in the ancient world, early Christians traveled a great deal. Such travel was motivated by the desire for "networking" among Christians, as well as by a desire to spread the gospel to new people groups. These travelers are likely the "strangers" whom our author mainly has in view—Christian missionaries from other cities and communities who needed somewhere to stay.

At that time, hospitality met this specific need and advanced the kingdom of God. But that is not all it involves. Hospitality is a central virtue for Christians (Romans 12:13; 1 Peter 4:9)—which is why it is given as a requirement for elders in the church (1 Timothy 3:2). It means looking out for the needs of others by welcoming them into your home.

In our day we easily confuse biblical hospitality with entertaining. Hospitality is not just about hosting dinner parties. It is more other-centered. It focuses on meeting a need rather than on having an enjoyable time. The motive is different.

This may mean inviting a different set of people to your home. Entertaining carries an expectation of reciprocity: if I invite someone to dinner, I will get invited back. It is just the way our social lives work. There is nothing wrong with that, but it is not what is being talked about here in Hebrews 13. This is welcoming strangers—inviting people for meals or to stay with us with no expectation that they will or even can reciprocate. This kind of hospitality can be inconvenient and hard; it requires a whole different level of focus and effort to welcome into your home those who are not already part of your social circle.

This concept of hospitality recalibrates the way we open up our homes; it is no longer just for our own pleasure but in order to advance the kingdom of God.

> It is significant that our author uses the word "remember." Honestly, it is easy to forget.

To drive home his point, our author offers the remarkable observation that some "have entertained angels unawares" (**v 2**). No doubt this is a reference to Genesis 18, where Abraham welcomes three strangers and gives them food and drink, and two of them turn out to be angels (the third being a **theophany** of the Lord himself); and to Genesis 19, where Lot welcomes the same two angels into his home to protect them from the dangerous citizens of Sodom.

The point here is not so much that we should expect angels in our homes today (though that is certainly possible) as that we just never know the significance our hospitality might have for the kingdom of God. A small act of kindness can have an immense impact.

## Loving Those in Prison

Next our author lays out a second example: "Remember those who are in prison, as though in prison with them, and those who are mistreated" (**v 3**).

Here again we have to understand the historical context. In this period, it was very common for Christians to be thrown into prison, not because they had committed a crime but merely for being Christians.

We read about this in a letter written to the Emperor Trajan by Pliny the Younger, who was a governor in a Roman province early in the second century (*Letters*, 10.96-97). Many Christians had stopped going to the pagan temples and worshiping the Roman gods. In an attempt to reverse this, Pliny tells the emperor that he has been arresting Christians and throwing them in jail. He tortured some and had some executed.

This kind of persecution was not unusual (for more information, see Bryan Litfin, *Early Christian Martyr Stories*). Christians would be thrown in jail, mistreated, mocked, arrested, and beaten; their money and livelihoods would be stolen. Caring for people in prison was therefore the need of the hour. The writer to the Hebrews is encouraging his readers to visit such Christians and care for their physical needs.

How do we translate that for the modern day? Certainly, some Christians are in prison now because they've committed a crime, and it would still be a good thing to go and visit them. We should show compassion to them also. But the principle that is mainly in view here is that we should help those Christians who are suffering innocently— those who have suffered persecution as a result of their faith.

It is significant that our author uses the word "remember." Honestly, it is easy to forget those who are being persecuted. We live in a culture that focuses on health, beauty, and success. Few want to think about those who lack these things. But we should be motivated to care for two reasons. First, we are effectively suffering with them. Look at the language used here: remember them "as though in prison with them." The reason we should care about them is that they are our spiritual brothers (**v 1**). If they hurt, we hurt. We are linked to them. "If one member suffers, all suffer together; if one member is honored, all rejoice together" (1 Corinthians 12:26).

Second, our author calls his audience to remember those who suffer for Christ because "you also are in the body" (Hebrews **13:3**). In other words, since all of us have physical bodies, we all have the potential to suffer physically. We should have compassion on those who are suffering because it could just as easily have been (and perhaps someday will be) us suffering.

## Look at Your Own Life

If **verses 1-3** have been about looking out for others, our author reminds us in **verses 4-6** that we should also be looking out for ourselves. The pursuit of holiness involves not only *external* considerations (caring for others) but also *internal* considerations (guarding our own lives).

Not surprisingly, the author chooses to focus on what are probably the two most common idols that human beings struggle with: sex and money.

He starts with sex: "Let marriage be held in honor among all" (**v 4**).

In our world today marriage is under attack in many ways—through the vast numbers of divorces, through people's unfaithfulness to their marriages, and through those who advocate many different versions of marriage.

It was a similar story when this letter was written. In the ancient world, sexual promiscuity was rampant and fairly well accepted in society. There was no expectation that men, in particular, would be faithful to their wives. So Christians were already distinctive in the way they viewed sex and marriage. The second-century Christian writer Tertullian, for example, said, "One in mind and soul, we do not hesitate to share our earthly goods with one another. All things are common among us *but our wives*" (*Apology*, 39; my italics).

Many tell us that God does not or should not really care about sex and marriage. "Doesn't God have bigger issues on his mind than what people do in their private sex lives?" they'll say—adding that, if you think the biblical view of sex and marriage matters, you're just a legalist—a Pharisee.

But God does care about these things. Faithful marriage between a man and a woman was designed by him. In Matthew 19:5-6 Jesus affirms marriage by quoting from Genesis: "Have you not read that he who created them from the beginning made them male and female, and said, 'Therefore a man shall leave his father and his mother and hold fast to his wife, and the two shall become one flesh'? ... What therefore God has joined together, let man not separate."

Honoring marriage is important partly because it is a picture of something bigger and greater. Ephesians 5 says that the relationship between a husband and wife is a picture of the way Christ loves the church. So if you dishonor marriage, you are dishonoring God's picture of redemption. That's a big issue.

There are other things at stake too. Disobeying God and doing whatever you want sexually has ramifications: broken homes, broken families, and many practical and psychological problems. I can speak to this on a pastoral level: at my church, the vast majority of big pastoral issues we deal with have something to do with people dishonoring God's plan for sex and marriage. God cares about sex and marriage because he cares about people.

Hebrews **13:4** also tells us that the reason we should hold marriage in honor is that "God will judge the sexually immoral and adulterous." That might be the most unpopular thing to say in our world today!

But we have to stick with what God says, even if it is unpopular. The reality is that God will judge sexual immorality.

That does not mean that there is no forgiveness for those of us who have sexual sin in our past or are struggling with sexual sin in the present. There is always forgiveness for those who repent of their sin, believe in Christ, and commit to living for him. It is the person who defies God directly and refuses to repent that God will judge for his or her sexual immorality.

Look at 1 Corinthians 6:9-11. Paul says, "Neither the sexually immoral, nor idolaters, nor adulterers, nor men who practice homosexuality ... will inherit the kingdom of God" (v 9-10). But in verse 11 he adds, "And such were some of you. But you were washed, you were sanctified, you were justified in the name of the Lord Jesus Christ and by the Spirit of our God." The message is that sexual sin is very serious; but if you repent and trust in Jesus, there is always forgiveness and grace.

We do not apply this verse by walking out in the world and condemning everybody who is sexually immoral. We start by applying it to our own lives. "Let the marriage bed be undefiled" (Hebrews **13:4**). Start by guarding your own marriage. Keep it pure. Do not let it slip away. That is the first thing to do.

## Don't Love Money

The next command has to do with money. "Keep your life free from love of money, and be content with what you have" (**v 5**).

Love of money is a big pitfall in the Christian life.

It is not sinful to have money. God sometimes blesses people with wealth. But do not think, therefore, that the love of money is not a danger that you need to be wary of. Money is like fire: it can keep you warm or it can burn your house down.

Of course, you don't have to be rich for this to be an issue. Poor people can love money. Even those who have nothing at all can covet what they don't have.

1 Timothy 6:9-10 describes the danger:

"Those who desire to be rich fall into temptation, into a snare, into many senseless and harmful desires that plunge people into ruin and destruction. For the love of money is a root of all kinds of evils. It is through this craving that some have wandered away from the faith and pierced themselves with many pangs."

Our author tells us that we need to "be content with what [we] have" instead of worrying about money. Why? Because God provides. The way you use money is a test of whether you really believe that. Do you hoard money for your own protection because you're afraid of what you might lose? Do you spend and spend, hoping that the next purchase will bring you a sense of security? Or are you content—not afraid of losing money or possessions but even able to give them away generously—because you know you have something far greater?

After all, God has said, "I will never leave you or forsake you" (Hebrews **13:5**; this is a quotation from Joshua 1:5). And "The Lord is my helper; I will not fear; what can man do to me?" (Hebrews **13:6**; this is a quotation from Psalm 118:6.) If you really do believe these things, you will not be so worried about money.

We need to be looking out for our own marriages and sexual behavior, and testing our own attitudes to money. Our author is not saying that if you get sex and money right, everything else in life will be perfect. He uses these big issues as examples. If we are to pursue holiness, we must do it proactively.

## Questions for reflection

1. How does this passage help you rethink hospitality? What are some practical steps you can take to do hospitality better?

2. What are some practical steps that can be taken to protect a person's marriage?

3. Why do you think money is such a key litmus test for our faith? How's your heart doing in regard to your love for money? What can you do to fight this idol?

## PART TWO

In the national parks of the United States, there are over 4,000 search-and-rescue missions every year. That means that thousands of times each year, hikers find themselves in real trouble. In certain parks there are dangerous animals: bears or mountain lions or snakes. Sometimes people get injured, maybe falling and breaking an ankle. Other times they get lost and end up having to spend the night outside, where they are in danger of hypothermia.

Most people who go out hiking are totally unprepared for these dangers. They don't realize how dangerous the wilderness and desert can really be.

The Christian life is not so different. We are on the way to our destination, but it is not an easy path. You can get distracted. You can get lost. You can get dragged off the path by false teachers. There are many dangers. How are you going to make it through that journey? You need to be prepared.

### Follow Your Guides

In the wilderness, a guide—someone who really knows the terrain and is equipped for the dangers—is the best help you can get. It is the same in the Christian life. The author brackets Hebrews **13:7-17** by telling us to listen to the guides God has provided us with: our leaders. Even though the word "church" is not used here, it is clearly church leaders who are in view: "those who spoke to you the word of God" (**v 7**).

Of course, we can (and should) study the Scriptures on our own; but this verse points to the central way that God wants us to learn about him: by hearing the word from our leaders. Preaching in the local church is the means God has especially appointed to deliver his word to his flock (2 Timothy 4:1-4). This is one reason why it is so important to be part of a regular congregation.

Leaders are also there as examples. We should "imitate their faith" (Hebrews **13:7**).

Elders and pastors do not just point out the path; they actually walk it in front of you. Of course, church leaders don't get everything right. But not being perfect is in fact one way that they can show us a good example. By repenting when they sin, they model what it looks like to be a sinner saved by grace, following Christ faithfully even when they fail.

In short, if leaders are striving to be like Christ, they can be worthy examples to follow. Paul explains it this way in 1 Corinthians 11:1: "Be imitators of me, as I am of Christ." In other words, *Insofar as I imitate Christ, imitate me.*

At the end of this passage, in Hebrews **13:17**, our author returns to the theme of church leaders once again. We are asked not only to pay attention to our leaders and imitate their faith but also to obey them as our shepherds.

In general in Western society, we don't like authority. We do not want to be told what to do. This is partly down to the rise of the internet and modern technology. You don't need a doctor; just go to WebMD. You don't need a stockbroker; just look at CNBC. As a society we do not believe we need experts.

But in the wilderness, and in the Christian life, you do need a guide.

If you have trouble submitting to church leaders, you are going to have a lot of trouble submitting to the Leader. You cannot say, *I'll submit to God, but I'm not going to submit to those he has appointed over me.* Submitting to one is like submitting to the other.

That said, we are not called to follow our leaders blindly. If they are taking you down a sinful or **heretical** path, then you should avoid them (more on this below). Moreover, some leaders are authoritarian and abusive, wielding their authority in a way that is for their own glory and power (1 Peter 5:3). Such leaders need to be exposed for the false shepherds that they are.

But most church leaders are faithful shepherds who are doing the best they can. And God puts those people in your life for a reason.

They are keeping watch over you "as those who will have to give an account" (Hebrews **13:17**). They bear a heavy burden in looking after you and leading you well. You should submit to them so that they can lead you "with joy and not with groaning."

## Watch Out for Danger

If you are going on the wilderness journey, you need more than a guide. You also need a realization that you are entering into a dangerous world. If you are going to make it, you need to be aware of the pitfalls. In the Christian life, false teachers are one such danger.

In New Testament times, there were all kinds of heresies attacking the church. Paul warns the Ephesian elders about this in Acts 20:29: "After my departure, fierce wolves will come in among you, not sparing the flock."

God's people are like sheep. There are a lot of different implications of that image, but one is that we are vulnerable. False teachers are like wolves that come in and drag a sheep off into the woods, never to be seen again. So our author says, "Do not be led away" (Hebrews **13:9**).

Some think that they can deal with false teaching by shutting themselves off from any non-Christian influences. But Paul also warns the elders of the Ephesian church, "From among your own selves will arise men speaking twisted things" (Acts 20:30). False teachers are not just *out there*. They are also *in here*, within the flock. That is what makes them so dangerous.

We once did a Sunday-school series at my church called "Bad Christian Books." Thousands of Christians are regularly reading popular books which say they are "Christian" but lead their readers down unbiblical paths. We offered the class because all Christians need to know about false teaching and to be able to spot it.

One way we recognize false teaching is simply by understanding that it is "strange" (Hebrews **13:9**) or new; it is not what the church has historically taught or what the Bible says. A teaching that is old is perhaps not as appealing as one that is new and shiny. But at the seminary where I teach, I often say, "We're happy to be unoriginal!" We should teach what Christians have always seen and found to be wonderful—and help people to see it again in fresh ways.

The fundamental reason why we should be wary of "new" teachings is because Jesus never changes. He is "the same yesterday and today and forever" (**v 8**).

To talk that way about Jesus is to affirm his divinity. Only God is the same yesterday, today, and forever. This eternality and unchanging nature sets Jesus apart from false teachers. He is a sure anchor that does not slip. He is consistent through the ages.

This is why we need to ask, first and foremost, what the Bible says about each teaching we encounter; and also what the church through the ages has said about it. If Jesus does not change, I should not embrace radical new teachings about him.


## Go to Jesus

There is one particular false teaching that our author wants his readers to see. This is the idea that what you eat is what makes you acceptable to God: "For it is good for the heart to be strengthened by grace, not by foods" (**v 9**).

What the author likely has in view here is what the whole book has had in view from the beginning, which is that certain teachers wanted the Jewish Christians to go back to the old ways of Judaism—including its laws about food. Our author is saying again what he has said all along: those days are over. The false teachers are likely telling people to eat certain kinds of food so that God will be pleased. But it is through Christ alone that we can become clean and acceptable to God.

All this is linked to the fact that the priests used to eat from the altar—they would eat certain parts of the animal sacrifices. But our author points to a better altar—one "from which those who serve the tent have no right to eat" (**v 10**).

The priests who served in the temple had the right to eat from the old altar. But they could not eat from the better altar that we have, because our sacrifice is the true one: we partake not in an animal but in Christ himself.

Next, the author shows us again how Christ is the fulfillment of those Old Testament sacrifices. When a sin offering was made, the priests would take the bodies of the sacrificial victims and burn them outside the camp (**v 11**). This was an important symbolic gesture. To be in the camp was to be near God; to be outside the camp was to be rejected by God. When animal sacrifices were put outside the camp, it was a symbolic picture of the fact that the judgment the people deserved had been diverted. The animals had been rejected outside the camp, so the people could stay inside the camp and draw near to God.

> The location of the cross reveals that Jesus was accomplishing what the animal sacrifices had pointed toward.

So it is significant that "Jesus also suffered outside the gate" (**v 12**).

When the Romans crucified Jesus, they did it outside the walls of Jerusalem. The location of the cross reveals the fact that Jesus was accomplishing what the animal sacrifices had pointed toward. He took on God's displeasure and was cast out of the city, taking the place of those who should have been rejected.

Therefore we are called to "go to him outside the camp and bear the reproach he endured" (**v 13**). Jesus took all this reproach and rejection for you. Are you willing to be associated with him? Are you willing to be associated with that sort of shame and humiliation?

Truthfully, we are all sometimes embarrassed by Jesus. We are embarrassed to be Christians and afraid of being looked at with ridicule or scorn. In the early church, as we have seen, Christians were enduring far more than mockery for their faith, as many believers around the world still are today. But our author is saying that this is worth enduring. Look at what Jesus has done for you! Because of him, we will never suffer rejection by God. Even if it means enduring scorn in this life, we need to join him.

After all, the communities we are part of here on earth are "no lasting city" (**v 14**). Instead "we seek the city that is to come." In other words, we want to go to the heavenly city: Zion, the new creation where we have been promised a safe place "inside the walls" and eternal fellowship with God. Jesus gets us in there. He was cast out of God's presence so that we could be with God forever.

And what should our response be to these great truths? The first is no surprise: "Let us continually offer up a sacrifice of praise to God, that is, the fruit of lips that acknowledge his name" (**v 15**). As we noted above (12:28), worship is always the most natural response to redemption. Curiously, our author refers to this worship as a "sacrifice," an analogy also made elsewhere in the New Testament (Romans 12:1; 1 Peter 2:5). Under the new covenant our sacrifices are no longer physical, but spiritual—the praise of our lips to the God who saved us.

The second response we should have to our redemption in Christ is to love one another, a theme already discussed above in Hebrews **13:1-3**. We are told, "Do not neglect to do good and to share what you have, for such sacrifices are pleasing to God" (**v 16**). Good works are the natural outflowing of the gospel of grace. Again, our author refers to these good works as a form of sacrifice, highlighting again the differences between the covenants. We don't sacrifice animals, but we sacrifice our lives.

## Closing Greetings

Hebrews does not begin like a typical Greco-Roman letter, as it lacks the traditional identification of the author. However, it does end like a standard letter, with closing appeals and greetings. Our author begins by making a personal request: "Pray for us, for we are sure that we have a clear conscience, desiring to act honorably in all things" (**v 18**). This request reveals the personal relationship between the author and his audience. The author wants them to know that his conscience is clean in regard to the letter he has written—it was done with honourable intentions and for their good. In addition, he needs the prayers of the congregation, primarily so that "I may be restored to you the sooner" (**v 19**). Obviously, the author is not merely delivering a cold, doctrinal treatise to this congregation; he genuinely loves them and wants to be with them.

We are not surprised, then, when in **verses 20-21** our author delivers a **benediction**, also a regular feature in the closing of letters (Romans 15:13; 1 Thessalonians 5:23; 2 Thessalonians 3:16). He clearly loves this congregation and desires to pronounce God's blessing upon them.

A number of themes from the letter are echoed in this benediction. He begins and ends it with Jesus, emphasizing his resurrection ("brought again from the dead") as well as his divine glory ("to whom be glory forever and ever"). The letter began with a similar focus on Jesus, particularly the truth that he was the "radiance of the glory of God" (Hebrews 1:3). Also, the benediction mentions "the blood of the eternal covenant": a clear nod to the nature of the new covenant as eternal and never-ending because it is built on the blood of a better sacrifice (see 9:13-15; 10:10; 12:24). And the focus on "pleasing" God by obedience to "his will" was already seen above in **13:16** as well as 11:5.

Then there are a few final statements and greetings. Our author asks that the congregation "bear with my word of exhortation" (**13:22**); that is, he wants them to listen to it and not cast it aside. The Timothy released from prison (**v 23**) may be the same Timothy to whom Paul wrote, suggesting that the author is part of the broader apostolic circle, though not necessarily an apostle himself. (See the

Introduction for more on this.) Then he closes the letter with greetings to "all your leaders and all the saints" (**v 24**)—an indication that he is writing to a real, local church with both leaders and a congregation, something he already hinted at in **verse 17**.

The last statement is a short blessing: "Grace be with all of you" (**v 25**). Similar endings are found in many other New Testament letters (1 Timothy 6:21; 2 Timothy 4:22; Titus 3:15; Philemon 25). But the theme of "grace" is a particularly fitting end to the book of Hebrews. The message of the book is that salvation is not earned by our efforts or merits, and certainly not through adherence to old-covenant ceremonies and rituals. Only the shed blood of the ultimate sacrifice, Jesus Christ, cleanses us. Only his blood enables us to "draw near to the throne of grace" (Hebrews 4:16).

## Questions for reflection

1. How does this passage help you in your view of church leaders?

2. What are some false teachings circulating in our world today?

3. How are you encouraged by Jesus enduring the rejection and judgment of God for you? What are some ways in which we can respond to that great gift?

# GLOSSARY

**Aaron:** Moses' brother; the first priest to serve in the tabernacle. Israel's priests were drawn from his descendants (see Exodus 28 – 29).

**Abram:** (or Abraham: he was called Abram until God changed his name in Genesis 17:5 to reflect the fact that he would be "the father of many nations.") The ancestor of the nation of Israel, and the man who God made a binding agreement (covenant) with. God promised to make his family into a great nation, give them a land, and bring blessing to all nations through one of his descendants (Genesis 12:1-3).

**Absolution:** declaration that a person's sins have been forgiven.

**Analogy:** a comparison between two things, usually using one of them to explain or clarify the other.

**Apostasy:** the abandonment of a religious belief or principle. An apostate is someone who once seemed to be a believer but who later totally rejects Christ, turns away from sound teaching, and leaves the church.

**Apostles:** men appointed directly by the risen Christ to teach about him with authority.

**Backsliding:** not living the Christian life as wholeheartedly as previously.

**Baptism:** a symbolic washing with water, either by sprinkling or total immersion, to reflect someone coming to faith in Christ and having their sin washed clean.

**Benediction:** blessing.

**Birthright:** in ancient Middle-Eastern cultures, the oldest son inherited the possessions (and sometimes position) of his father.

**Church discipline:** the practice of reprimanding church members when they are perceived to have sinned in hope that the offender will repent and be reconciled to God and the church. It is also intended to protect other church members from the influence of sin.

**Commentator:** the author of a commentary, a book that explains parts of the Bible verse by verse.

**Common grace:** good things which God gives regardless of whether someone is a Christian or not (e.g. rain, oxygen).

**Cornerstone:** a stone that forms the base of a corner of a building, joining two walls.

**Covenant:** a binding agreement between two parties.

**Covenant line:** the family line of Abraham, with whom the Lord made his covenant—Abraham, Isaac, and Jacob.

**Day of Atonement:** the one day in the year when the high priest could enter the Most Holy Place in the tabernacle/temple to make a sacrifice on behalf of the people (Leviticus 16).

**Denominations:** different branches of the church (e.g. Presbyterian, Southern Baptist, Anglican/Episcopalian, Methodist).

**Destroyer of the firstborn:** in the book of Exodus, God rescued his people from slavery in Egypt through sending plagues. In the final plague, the Lord sent "the destroyer" (Exodus 12:23) to kill the first-born in every family. This could be avoided only by killing a lamb in the firstborn's place so that God's judgment would "pass over" that household (see Exodus 12 – 13).

**Devotional life:** regularly praying and reading the Bible.

**Doctrine/Doctrinal:** doctrines are statements of what is true about God.

**Elders:** men who are responsible for the teaching and ministry of a church.

**Evangelicals/Evangelicalism:** Christians who emphasize the Bible's authority and the need to be personally converted through faith in Jesus' death and resurrection.

**Exodus:** literally "way out" or "departure"; the historical period when the people of Israel left slavery in Egypt and began to travel toward the promised land (i.e. the events recounted, unsurprisingly, in the book of Exodus).

**Fruit of the Spirit:** the characteristics that the Holy Spirit grows in Christians, including love, joy, peace, patience, kindness, goodness, faithfulness, gentleness and self-control (see Galatians 5:22-23).

**Gnostics:** the name for various religious groups in the first centuries AD. They thought that the material world was evil and denied that Jesus was really human.

**Grace:** unmerited favor. In the Bible, "grace" is usually used to describe how God treats his people. Because God is full of grace, he gives believers eternal life (Ephesians 2:4-8); he also gives them gifts to use to serve his people (Ephesians 4:7, 11-13).

**Heretical:** a belief which directly opposes the biblical gospel (i.e. the opposite of orthodox). A heretic is someone who, despite being challenged, continues to hold to heretical beliefs.

**Incarnation:** the coming of the divine Son of God as a human, in the person of Jesus Christ.

**Inspired:** divine inspiration is the belief that all of the Bible was inspired by God, so that the humans writing the words wrote exactly what he intended them to (see 2 Timothy 3:15-17; 2 Peter 1:20-21).

**Intercede:** speak on behalf of someone in difficulty or trouble.

**Intercessor:** someone who speaks on behalf of someone else to help them. Jesus intercedes on our behalf to God the Father.

**Isaac:** one of the **patriarchs**.

**Jacob:** one of the **patriarchs**.

**Joseph:** The second-youngest son of Jacob, and the great-grandson of Abraham. He was the first of Abraham's family to live in Egypt; the rest of the family followed him there, and in subsequent generations were enslaved.

**Joshua:** leader of the people of Israel after Moses. One of only two people who were both rescued from slavery in Egypt and also set foot in the promised land of Canaan.

**Judah:** in this context, one of the sons of Jacob. God promised that the Messiah would come from the family line (tribe) of Judah.

**Justification:** the declaration that someone is not guilty, not condemned, completely innocent.

**Law/The law:** the books of Exodus, Leviticus, Numbers and Deuteronomy, which include laws about how the people of Israel were to relate to God and live as his people.

**Lazarus:** brother of Mary and Martha, whom Jesus brought back to life (John 11:38-44).

**Loins:** in this context, the region of the sexual organs.

**Lord's Supper:** or Communion: sharing bread and wine together to remember the body and blood of Jesus.

**Manna:** the "bread" that God miraculously provided each morning for the Israelites to eat while they were journeying to the promised land (see Exodus 16). It looked like white flakes.

**Man of God:** servant of God; a Christian.

**Mediate:** act as a go-between for two parties in a dispute.

**Messiah:** Christ, the anointed one. In the Old Testament, God promised that the Messiah would come to rescue and rule his people.

**Minister:** one who serves; in this context, Jesus serves by mediating on our behalf with God the Father.

**Moses:** the leader of God's people at the time when God brought them out of slavery in Egypt. God communicated his law (including the Ten Commandments) through Moses, and under his leadership guided them toward the land he had promised to give them.

**Objectively:** not influenced by feelings or opinions.

**Papacy:** the office or authority of the Pope.

**Patriarch:** the "first fathers" of Israel, to whom God gave his promises—Abraham, Isaac and Jacob.

**Pharisees:** a Jewish group who lived by strict observance of both God's

Old Testament law and Jewish tradition. They mistakenly thought their law-observance made them right with God.

**Philistines:** ancient enemies of the Israelites.

**Proof text:** Bible passage used to prove a teaching point.

**Puritan:** a member of a sixteenth and seventeenth-century movement in Great Britain which was committed to the Bible as God's word, to simpler worship services, to greater commitment and devotion to following Christ, and increasingly to resisting the institutional church's hierarchical structures. Many emigrated to what would become the US, and were a strong influence on the church in most of the early colonies.

**Redeemer/Redemption:** the act of redeeming, or releasing, sinners. In Bible times, one could redeem a slave by paying their owner the full price for their release. By dying on the cross, Jesus paid the penalty for sin to release Christians from slavery to sin, death and judgment (see Romans 3:23-25; Ephesians 1:7).

**Redemptive history:** the process throughout history by which God has and will rescue his people from sin to live in relationship with him forever.

**Regenerate:** born again; made spiritually alive through the work of the Spirit at the point of putting faith in Jesus Christ.

**Remission of sins:** forgiveness; redemption.

**Revival:** reawakening of religious fervor.

**Sabbath:** Saturday; the holy day when Jewish people were commanded not to work (see Exodus 20:8-11).

**Saints:** all Christians.

**Samaritans:** people from the region of Samaria; a people group with mixed Jewish-pagan ancestry and religion.

**Samuel:** a prophet who led Israel before the reign of King Saul.

**Sanctify:** make holy or make more like Christ, by the work of the Holy Spirit.

**Saul:** here, the first king of Israel (see 1 Samuel 8 – 10).

**Sovereign:** having supreme authority / being the supreme ruler.

**Subjective:** something which is based on feelings and opinions; e.g. "She is the most beautiful woman in the world" is a subjective opinion.

**Supplications:** earnest prayers.

**Tabernacle:** a large, tented area where the Israelites worshiped God, and where his presence symbolically dwelled (see Exodus 26; 40).

**The body of Christ:** Christians; the church.

**Theological:** focusing on God's perspective and the truth about him.

**Theology:** the study of the truth about God.

**Theophany:** visible manifestation of God.

**Theses:** statements.

**Tithe:** here, referring to the Old Testament command to give a tenth of one's possessions to the work of God.

**Transgressions:** sins. Literally, the word means "stepping across a line."

**Trials:** testing periods of life; e.g. a time of ill-health, or persecution, or loneliness, or unemployment.

**Types:** people or events in the Old Testament that foreshadow someone or something in the New Testament.

**Visible church:** the communities and organizations in which God's people gather and can be seen by others, contrasted with the totality of God's people throughout history and worldwide.

**Wrath:** God's settled, right, and deserved hatred of and anger at sin.

# BIBLIOGRAPHY

- Richard Baxter, *The Saints' Everlasting Rest* (Epworth Press, 1962)

- John Frame, *The Doctrine of the Word of God* (P&R, 2010)

- C.S. Lewis, *The Last Battle* (HarperCollins, 1956)

- C.S. Lewis, *The Screwtape Letters* (Macmillan, 1961)

- C.S. Lewis, *The Problem of Pain* (Macmillan, 1962)

- Bryan Litfin, *Early Christian Martyr Stories* (Baker Academic, 2014)

- Martin Luther, *Luther's Works,* translated by John W. Doberstein (Fortress, 1959)

- Tertullian, *Apology*, English translation from A. Roberts and J. Donaldson, eds., *The Ante-Nicene Fathers* (Hendrickson, 1885)

# THE WHOLE SERIES

- **Exodus For You**
  Tim Chester

- **Judges For You**
  Timothy Keller

- **Ruth For You**
  Tony Merida

- **1 Samuel For You**
  Tim Chester

- **2 Samuel For You**
  Tim Chester

- **Psalms For You**
  Christopher Ash

- **Proverbs For You**
  Kathleen Nielson

- **Daniel For You**
  David Helm

- **Micah For You**
  Stephen Um

- **Luke 1-12 For You**
  Mike McKinley

- **Luke 12-24 For You**
  Mike McKinley

- **John 1-12 For You**
  Josh Moody

- **John 13-21 For You**
  Josh Moody

- **Acts 1-12 For You**
  Albert Mohler

- **Acts 13-28 For You**
  Albert Mohler

- **Romans 1-7 For You**
  Timothy Keller

- **Romans 8-16 For You**
  Timothy Keller

- **2 Corinthians For You**
  Gary Millar

- **Galatians For You**
  Timothy Keller

- **Ephesians For You**
  Richard Coekin

- **Philippians For You**
  Steven Lawson

- **Colossians & Philemon For You**
  Mark Meynell

- **1 & 2 Timothy For You**
  Phillip Jensen

- **Titus For You**
  Tim Chester

- **Hebrews For You**
  Michael Kruger

- **James For You**
  Sam Allberry

- **1 Peter For You**
  Juan Sanchez

- **Revelation For You**
  Tim Chester

Find out more about these titles at:

# www.thegoodbook.com/for-you

**BIBLICAL | RELEVANT | ACCESSIBLE**

At The Good Book Company, we are dedicated to helping Christians and local churches grow. We believe that God's growth process always starts with hearing clearly what he has said to us through his timeless word—the Bible.

Ever since we opened our doors in 1991, we have been striving to produce Bible-based resources that bring glory to God. We have grown to become an international provider of user-friendly resources to the Christian community, with believers of all backgrounds and denominations using our books, Bible studies, devotionals, evangelistic resources, and DVD-based courses.

We want to equip ordinary Christians to live for Christ day by day, and churches to grow in their knowledge of God, their love for one another, and the effectiveness of their outreach.

Call us for a discussion of your needs or visit one of our local websites for more information on the resources and services we provide.

Your friends at The Good Book Company

thegoodbook.com | thegoodbook.co.uk
thegoodbook.com.au | thegoodbook.co.nz
thegoodbook.co.in